DISPATCHES
FROM THE FOB

Published by Lit Riot Press, LLC
Brooklyn, NY
www.litriotpress.com

Book and cover design by Ben Taylor

Names: Adkins, Paul, 1962-
Title: Dispatches From The FOB / Paul David Adkins.
Description: Lit Riot Press, 2018. | Summary: Dispatches From the
    FPB. | 978-0-9992943-4-5 (pbk.)
Subjects: BISAC: POETRY / General. | POETRY / American /
    General. | POETRY / Subjects & Themes / General. | HISTORY
    / Military / Iraq War (2003-2011). | HISTORY / Middle East
    / Iraq. | HISTORY / Modern / 21st Century. | LITERARY
    COLLECTIONS / American / General.

DISPATCHES FROM THE FOB

A POETRY ANTHOLOGY

PAUL DAVID ADKINS

LIT RIOT PRESS

BROOKLYN, NEW YORK

FM 101-5-1 MCRP 5-2A

OPERATIONAL TERMS AND GRAPHICS

*I want to thank the following people for their
assistance with this book
my wife Melanie who shared this project
with me;
my children Ellen Leone, Martha Gray, Lily
Talitha, and Malachi Ray;
my forerunner Lynn Butler Schiffhorst;
my editor Kelli Russell Agodon;
my Army buddy Danielle Palace Blanco;
my blurb writers Katie Ford, Lynn Butler
Schiffhorst, and Joanie Stangeland;
the editors who took a chance and "tossed
my Paxil;"
the poets whose work inspired this collection;*

No soldier says, "We let the wounded die."
He says, *There was one I recall*
we took to the hospital and treated. He says

I saw the column of smoke,
but not the fire.

-- Susan Tichy, "Inheritance: The Water
Cure, part two,"
A Smell of Burning Starts the Day

TABLE OF CONTENTS

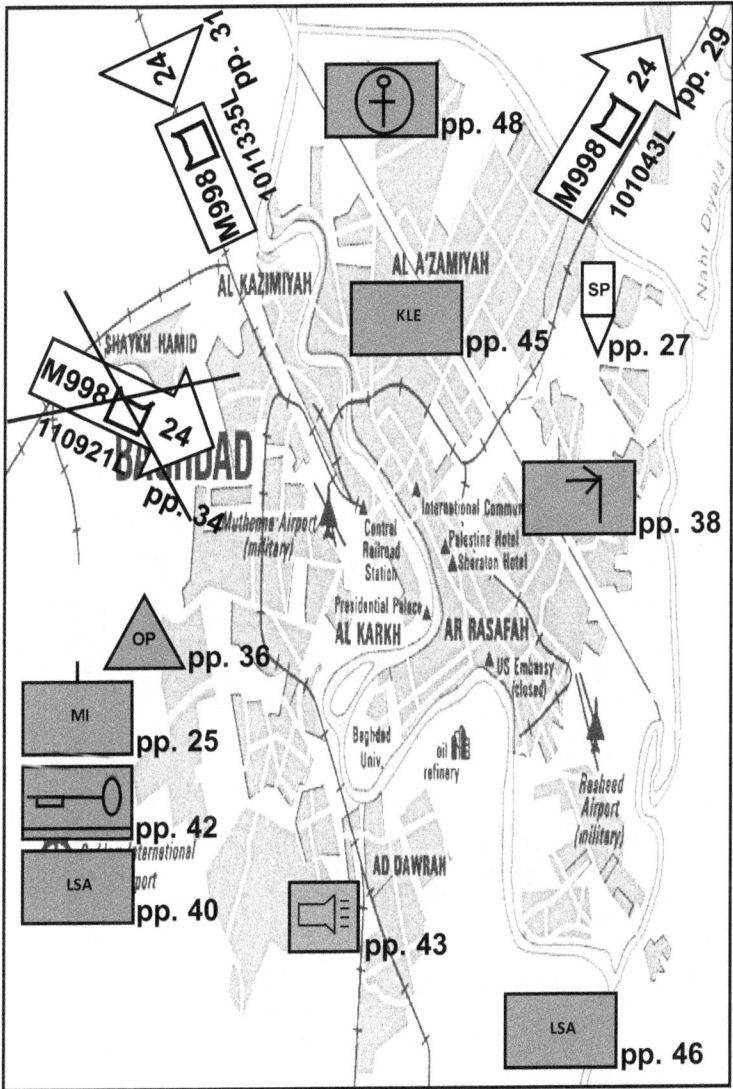

TABLE OF CONTENTS

TABLE OF CONTENTS

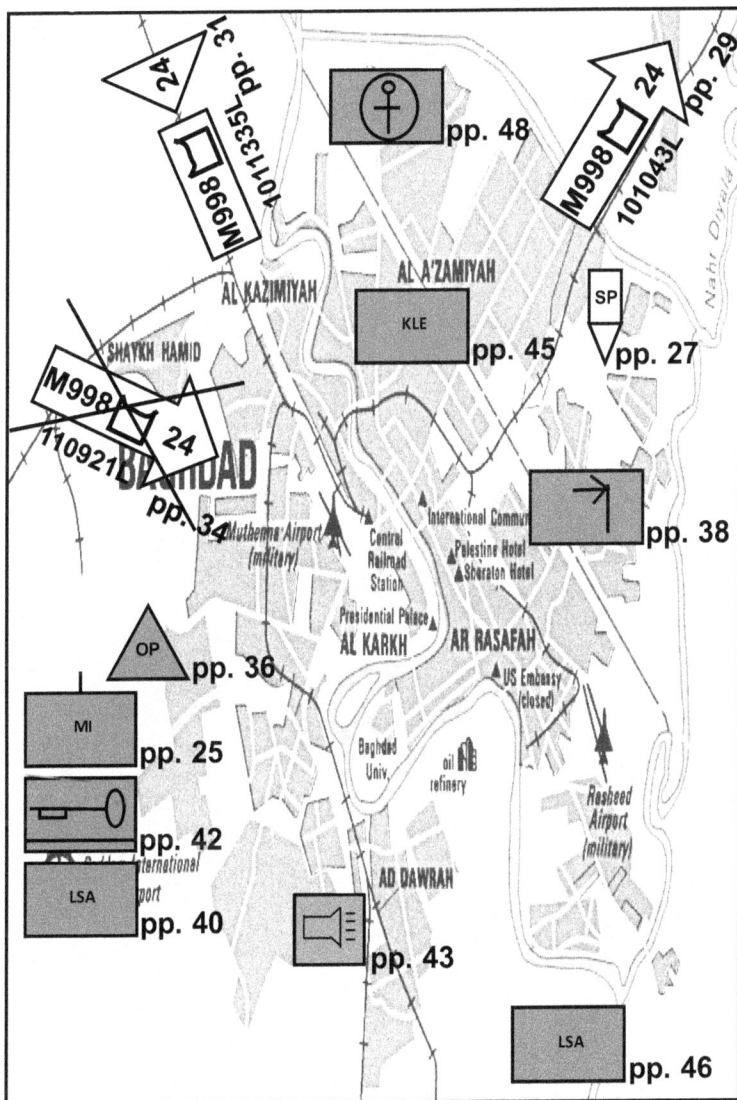

INTRODUCTION

To the enthusiast of military history, a good map tells everything: contour, overlook, reverse slope, avenue of approach, impassible obstacle. The unit symbols denote marches, routes, defenses, strong-points. And yet, to the layman, the onlooker, the casual observer, they stand without value. They inherently cannot represent what is really happening on the battlefield to the single-most important element: the combatant.

In *Operational Terms and Graphics*, I hope to divulge the human struggles beneath the symbols and designs: the struggles, the slaughter, the fear, the boredom, the hatred, and the torching that war lays upon the human spirit. Hence, I couple the maps and symbols with corresponding human experiences to counter the reporting of events so coldly depicted otherwise in news outlets, social media sites, memes, and sound bites. While I am not so naïve to think my poetry can singlehandedly stem the tide of profession-ally-crafted propaganda, bald-eagle posters, and war-glorifying movies, I am responsible, required, to add my voice to the debate, even a single dissenting text to oppose the hyper-patriotic, the ignorant, and the overwhelming proponency of war. Ice Cube famously claimed while a member of the band NWA, "Yo, Dre, I got something to say!" And so do I, as a soldier, a veteran, to my country and the world.

Many poets have employed their talents to warn us about this blood sport called war: Alan Seeger, Louis Simpson, Yusuf Komunyakaa, Karen Skolfield, and Harvey Shapiro, to name a few. And, accompanying the resonance of these masters, I ring the tiny chalice of my bell, to punctuate and highlight one soldier's experiences during President Bush's wars. I cannot speak for anyone else. But, "Insha'allah," Arabic for "God willing," I will speak clearly, concisely, precisely – a rifle shot, descending mortar round, incoming rocket – perfectly on point.

ACKNOWLEDGEMENTS

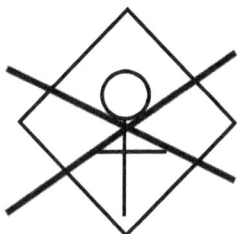

("Baghdad Murder: Kneeling Man")
Published as "War Story # 80: Baghdad
Murder – Kneeling Man," *River Oak
Review*

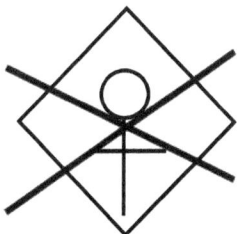

("Beheading Event") Published as "War
Story # 105: Beheading Event, Sunni
Triangle, Iraq," *Chiron Review*

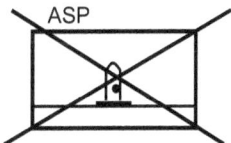

("Burning Ammunition Supply Point")
Published as "War Story # 63: Burning
Ammo Dump," *Hiram Poetry Review*

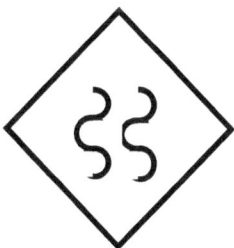

("Disappearance of Margaret Hassan,
UNICEF Aid Worker") Published as
"Disappearance of Margaret Hassan,
UNICEF Aid Worker, Baghdad, Iraq,"
Handsome Journal

("Dragging Hussein Palace Recreational Lake for Bodies") Published as "War Story # 104: Dragging Hussein Palace Lake for Bodies," *Concho River Review*

("Finding a Bone on FOB Hammer, Iraq") Published as "War Story # 137: A Bone on FOB Hammer," *Earth's Daughters*

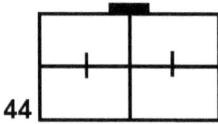

("44th Field Hospital, Christmas, 2003") Published as "44th Field Hospital at Christmas -- Bagram, AFG," *Crab Creek Review*

("Fruit Stand") Published as "War Story # 54: Fruit Stand," *Caveat Lector*

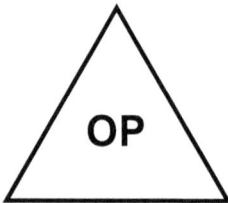

("Guard Tower Overlooking Ameriyah, Baghdad") *Pif*

("Hatred") Published as "War Story #27: Hatred," *94 Creations*

("Helicopter Flyover, Saba al-Boor") Published as "War Story # 103: Helicopter Flyover," *Red Rock Review*

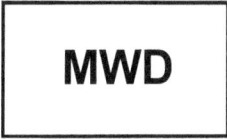

("Helicopter Ride with Cadaver Dog") Published as "War Story # 133: Helicopter Ride with Cadaver Dog," *Rattle*

("Humanitarian Assistance: Potable Water Delivery"), *Viral Cat*

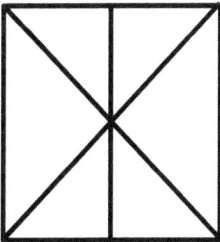

("Iraqi Army Unit on Camp Striker, Baghdad, Iraq"), *Scintilla*

("Iraqi Barber on FOB Hammer") Published as "War Story # 113: Iraqi Barber on a U.S. Base," *Borderline*

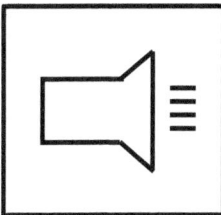

("Iraqi Girl with Prosthetic Hands") Published as "War Story # 76: Iraqi Girl with Prosthetic Hands," *Borderline*

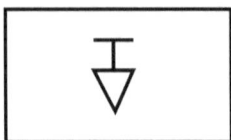

("Kings") Published as "War Story # 119: Kings," *Diode*

("Man in Suicide Vest") Published as "War Story # 8: Man in Suicide Vest," *Madison Review*

("Marking VBIEDs") Published as "Marking V-BIEDs in Iraq," *Border Crossing*

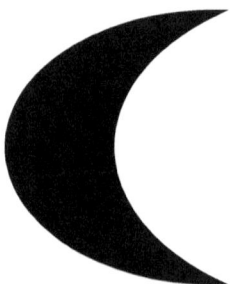

("Mosque Monitoring") Published as "War Story # 25: Mosque Monitoring," *Artful Dodge*

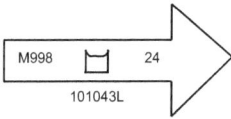

("Mourning") Published as "My Son," *Operation Homecoming*, Carroll, A., ed. Random House, NY, 2006, pp. 234-5

M998   24
101043L

("Passing the Flags") Published as "War Story # 124: Passing of the Flags," *Sierra Nevada Review*

APOE

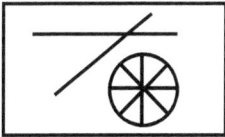

("Kings") Published as "War Story # 119: Kings," *Diode*

SP

("Prayer Before Conducting Convoy Operations") Published as "War Story # 33: Prayer Before Entering Iraq," *Ancient Paths*

K

("Search for Kidnapping Victims, Radwaniyah") Published as "War Story # 43: Search for Kidnapping Victims, Radwaniyah, Iraq," *Pif*

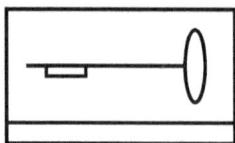

("Sew Shop, Log Base Seitz, Camp Victory, Iraq") Published as "Sew Shop – Bagram, AFG," *FEAST*

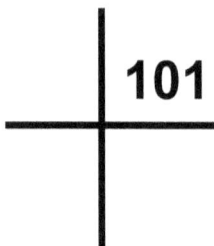

("Tree of Woe") Published as "War Story # 13: Tree of Woe," *Pearl*

APOD

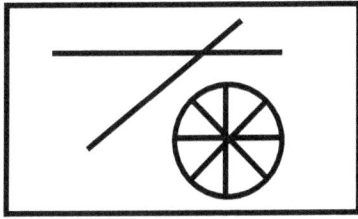

LEAVING THE UNITED STATES
FOR IRAQ: DECEMBER, 2006

Slow as bergs the buses bobbed
through the snow curtains,
away from the unit
and families who waved and
heard from the captain that
no one
could follow them further.

Onto roads scraped flat
and salted gray, the buses lurched
into the current,
the inevitable draw
of the airfield.

MPs led them with flashers
and sirens.

The line ran stop lights

as though each bus was a long hearse.

No one spoke.
We swayed with the rhythm
of potholes,
chop of railroad tracks.
The wipers groaned
like stressed planks

Our rifles,
black forearms of iron,
those motionless rowers.

We closed our eyes

until a minivan blew past,
flashing its brights,
honking and drifting as
the driver peered
into each bus window
for her husband,

waving and waving
like a drowning sailor,

and yelling and
yelling my name.

MI

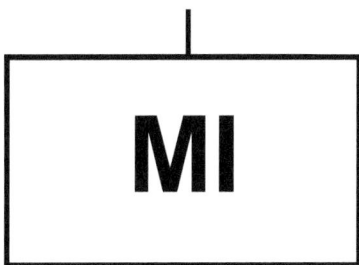

MILITARY INTELLIGENCE

I did not see bodies,
blood nor burning trucks.
I did not brush aside
shrieking women in the flaming market
nor ignore their sobbing children.

I stayed on the FOB.

But I knew.

I did not see
but knew the way
I knew what happened
in the room next door
in college.

I did not need to see
the swollen eye
to know a blow was dealt.

I heard the smack.

I deciphered breaking glass,
knew two lovers fought.

I knew he forced her -- how she screamed,
stopped screaming.
I did not have to watch the hand
shutter the mouth.
It was none of my affair.

But I knew.

And I don't have to tell you.

But I will.

Because if I don't
I am the door
which withstood
the butting shoulder,
pounding fists.

SP

PRAYER BEFORE CONDUCTING
CONVOY OPERATIONS

The convoy gathered --
Humvees, Hemmets, five tons.
Some bristled machine guns.
Mine? We cradled M-16s.

Our checks complete, weapons clean,
the rucksacks padded bumpers.
-- *We SP at zero-six.* --
Gunners played cards on a cooler.
Drivers sat cursing, then laughed.
Day slipped from the shell.

I walked
the line of trucks in fading light,
touched each

in Jesus' name.
I prayed for safety,
homecoming outside of a box.
Everyone -- survive.

I prayed
like Mother taught.

Keep us until the morning
light. No dying
before we wake.
Not a single
soul to take.

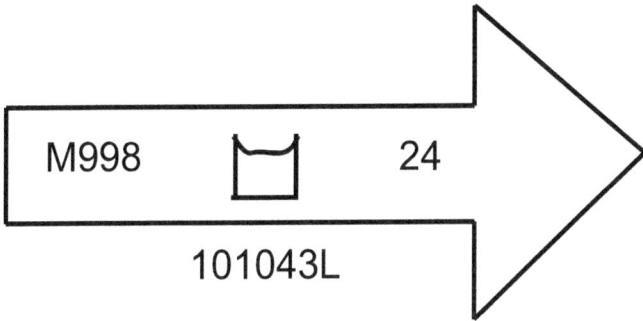

```
  M998      ⊔      24
        101043L
```

MOURNING

Three weeks before, I kissed my son
goodbye. Now, I was patrolling
        somewhere
in Iraq on a convoy,
the desert gritting in sun,
that torch of sand
and wind.

My son cried and cried
that day. No one
told him. No milk
or cake sufficed. He knew
I was dead. I
had left him forever

like a balloon that slipped
from his fingers.
I was floating

               somewhere
alone. And he

was finally turning away,
to toddle from that spot
where he lost me, finally not
craning at that patch of sky
where he had last
seen me waving
before I lifted
from his hand.

```
 _____                    /|
|                   |                  / |
|  M998    ⊔        |<────────        /  |
|_____|          \     / 24|
        101335L                 \   /    |
                                 \ /     |
                                  V_____|
```

M998   101335L   24

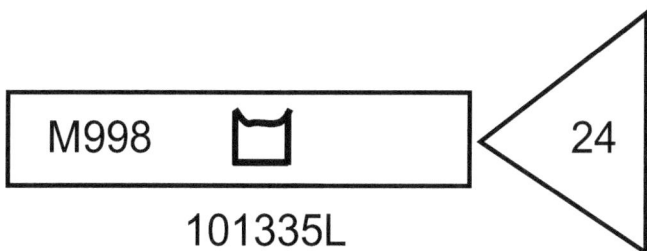

THE PONCHO LINERS WE USED
BETWEEN SCANIA AND MOSUL

At hour-six of an all-day convoy drive up Highway
    One,
we didn't stop.

We drank
more water.
It was noon --
one hundred twenty degrees.
We sweated through our IBA.

I balanced out
the Humvee door
on a stretch of road
that looked bump-free,
and peed.

A soldier in the back seat
contorted,

rocking.

She almost
        cried *Thank God*
when we halted
for an IED
spotted by a Bradley
five miles to our front.

The men
stretched and popped
their flies to face
the open desert.

My driver yanked
poncho liners out.
We hoisted
a makeshift blind.
She burst inside.

        Damnshitbitch!

A button butted my boot.
We tiptoed to avoid
the spreading puddle. We
held what we got.

        Hey, Garcia,
the driver laughed,

        Who wrote the novel
        Yellow River?

Shut
the fuck up!

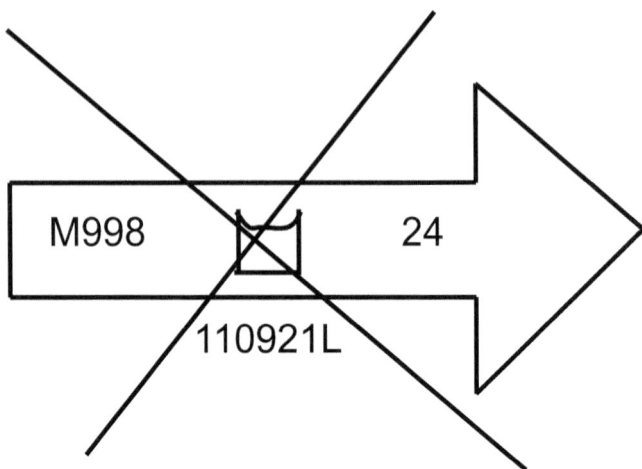

BURNING CONVOY

It's not enough
a Humvee burns,
an American dead in the cab.

It's not enough
a crowd gathers
waving arms and AKs.
They sing and push
at a camera crew,

torch and stamp an American flag.
It's not enough
that a boy spies a dying soldier cringing
in a nearby thicket, runs to his father.

It's not enough
the father follows the boy
back to the soldier, throws him over his shoulder.
The crowd cheers,
clears a path.
The man half-staggers,

half-sprints to the still-burning truck.
He heaves the soldier in.
No one shoots

at the screaming.

The mob flees as tanks approach.
The tanks engage
a slow-footed drunk.
It's not enough.

There's no sound now but idling tanks,
dying flames and *thwock*
of a black helmet
falling from the Humvee
to the seething concrete.

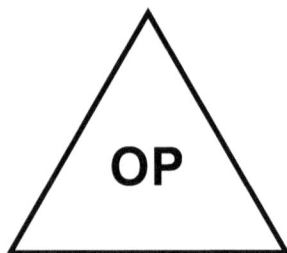

GUARD TOWER OVERLOOKING AMERIYAH, BAGHDAD

One hundred twenty steps, twelve flights
    to enter a stifling room
        containing radio, machine gun, table, two
        chairs.

The soldiers sat for hours,
    for weeks. The city beneath them
        indifferent with lovers,
        vandals, broken glass.

Finally they figured
    Who cares,

shucked body armor, pants.

One in the chair,
    one on the floor. One on the floor,
        one in the chair.

They turned up the radio
        inside their swaying cell,

its door firmly locked,
        guns in hand.

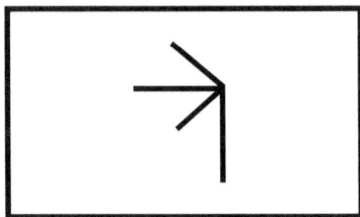

PASSING THE FLAGS

Throughout the shower trailer,
amid the steam and hiss
and shaving men
hung towels of every color.

The Army issued brown terry.
We buried
those spares in duffel bags
deep as tulip bulbs.

But in the trailer -- yellow bath,
lime green beach, purple,
chartreuse hand.
Sky blue, orange,
even a pink washcloth

-- *Excuse me -- it's salmon.*

Ten minutes every day
we stripped our O.D., brown,
black and tan to human flesh,

and rinsed.

Above us sagged
our plain and brilliant flags.

They still whiffed of fabreze,
folded by our solemn
wives and mothers
before they passed
them to us, weeping.

```
LSA
```

A BONE ON FOB HAMMER, IRAQ

Near HQ the soldier found a length of bone,
bagged it,
queried medics.

They shrugged –

> *Human tibia.*
> *This desert*
> *is covered*
> *in bones.*
>
> *Return it where it lay*
> *and wash your hands.*

She slipped it in a coffee can,
bore it to her room,
pondered it
like Yorick's skull.

She feared a ghost
would serenade the bone,

feared the bone
would claw the can
like a frantic mouse.

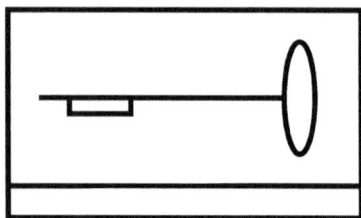

SEW SHOP, LOG BASE SEITZ, CAMP LIBERTY, IRAQ

Seven men huddled, all dishdashas and scarves,
by the heater and stacked, tan uniforms.
They chatted in Bangla.

Another man raced a modern Singer roughshod
around an American flag sleeve patch.
A boy sat behind a flat black table
straightening papers. It was like a barber shop --

lots of talk, a little work. On a radio
a sitar-woman wailed
what seemed like Indian music.
Her voice bobbed and floated --

a huge hummingbird. An American boss
briskly entered -- *Jesus Christ!* -- snapped off the radio
and left. No one spoke. The Singer growled,
hemmed in another flag.

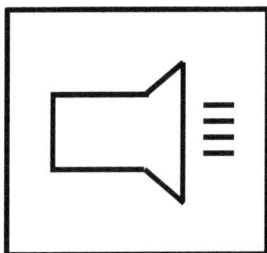

IRAQI GIRL WITH PROSTHETIC HANDS

What could I think of air turned fire?

The pressure of the blast,
waking with no hands
when earlier I had carried candy.

It has been years -- first stumps
then hooks.

I have learned some things:
using spoons, turning pages.
I can write twelve letters, even words.

I can wrap a scarf.

It's the future which worries me.
Who would marry a woman without hands?

On our wedding night, what would my husband think?

What could he possibly think
when I latch my hooks
around his naked hips, weep?

```
KLE
```

CHAI

Mother uttered certain sayings --
> *Sticks and stones may break my bones . . .*
> *Do unto others . . .*

Every occasion, every slight
ushered a homily.

An Iraqi served me chai,
bore chipped china on a tin tray.

He dunked a lump of sugar,
stirred it with his pinkie.

I peered into the whorl,
recalled,
> *Drink deep*
> *from the draught you've been drawn.*

LSA

IRAQI BARBER ON FOB HAMMER

I can't strangle Americans.
I need the job.

I noticed soldiers rush.

No time, no time

for a shave, an eyebrow trim.

Once seated, they're mine.

They wince.
I work the alcohol
into their open pores.

I clip and snip.

They tap fingernails
against the armrests –

trigger-clicks
on empty guns.

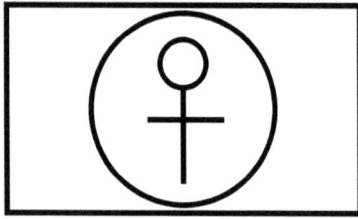

RESISTANCE

After the raid,
a blindfolded Iraqi sat
zip tied by the Humvees.

Two guards pointed M-4s his way
and prayed
-- Please
jump and try to run.

The prisoner shifted, settled.

Officers approached.
The terp barked.
The prisoner rose slowly, groaned.

A guard snatched the blindfold.
An officer readied and pointed
a camera. They wanted a picture
for records. The flash snapped
just as the prisoner stuck
his tongue out,
bugged his bloodshot eyes.

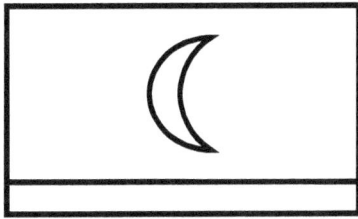

HUMANITARIAN ASSISTANCE:
POTABLE WATER DELIVERY

Americans delivered two pallets of water bottles
to the squalid town --
from a distance,
crystal cubes.

Boys ran up to heave
this shimmer home
to beaming mothers.

But teenage hoodlums
waved them down to play
Bomb the Americans

in the open sewer
behind a burned hospital.
They launched the bottles

into the swill
one by one by two by six . . .
Eight thousand bottles bobbed.

Ankle-deep,
the commander glared
as laughing boys danced by.

DISAPPEARANCE OF
MARGARET HASSAN, UNICEF
AID WORKER

Not a shadow left
of her. All
that remained
were scuffs
in dust.

In days ahead
across the town,
tacked on light poles,
her photo

-- Have you seen her? --

defiled with
ink goatee,
devil horns,
eyes poked out.

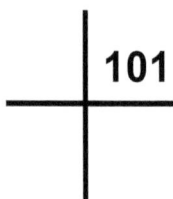

101

TREE OF WOE

The only roadside oak for miles.
Dark stains orbited the trunk
for fifty yards -- acorns
crushed by cars.

Insurgents used the tree to aim their IEDs.
Fifty meters past the trunk
place bomb. Based on convoy speed,
they knew when to set it off --

first truck, last,
in between. Whenever the bomber
chose.

We figured it out two months
in the fight. We cut the tree

to roots. Its branches stretched,
dead hands. Next day
with chainsaws, soldiers severed limb
from trunk,

cut trunk to misshapen *O*'s.
They hauled it in three trucks.
They entombed the stump in concrete.

Next day from the cement sprouted
a green, ten-foot tall, reinforcing rod.

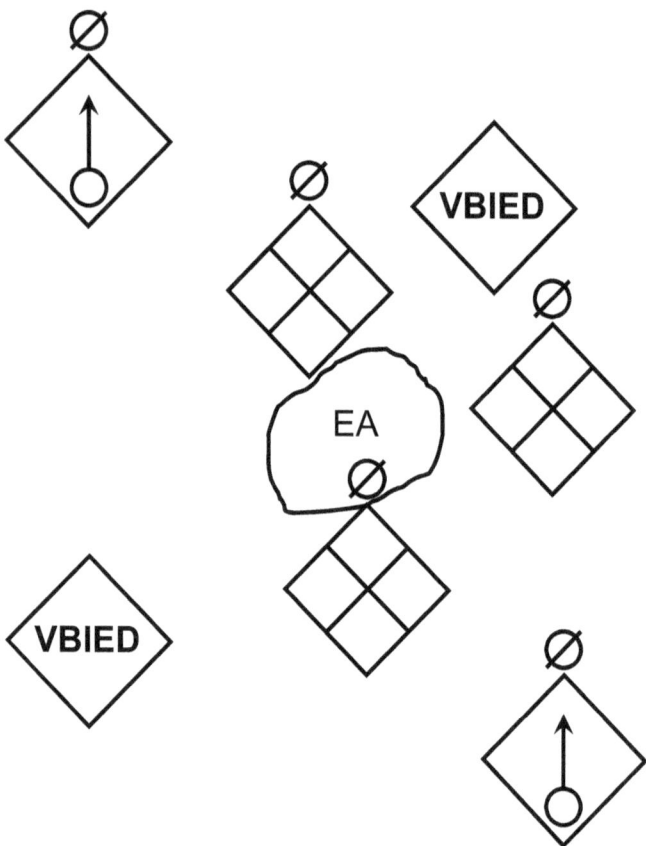

COORDINATED ENEMY ATTACK
ON A PRISON

We heard VBIEDs strike far off,
ten in a two-hour span --
. . . *What on Earth?*

Then the raid. Inmates rose in concert.
Infantry tossed grenades over walls.   Coordinated
    mortars.

Then,

all clear. The courtyard pocked
with craters. Spent brass
strewn across the guard tower floors.
Flat layers of smoke floated
grainy as a home movie.

Next day
we analyzed maps, saw VBIEDs

isolated the target.
Everything
tied in. Car bombs boxed the camp.

Like clippings in folded paper
revealed through unraveling

an intricate star,
descending flare.

SVIED

MAN IN SUICIDE VEST

In line to vote, his coat hid the vest.

But just part
of the bomb blew,
and he killed only
himself.

A few minor wounds nearby,
some singed beards
and brows.

The injured pressed
cloths to cuts,
stepped back
in line.

Moving forward, they
stared
at the bomber dead
on the ground.

Then someone jumped
out, stamped the body.

Suddenly, dozens
smacked it with shoes.
They cursed and spat.
Frenzied kicking
and hacks.

The head shot off. Cheers.
A young man booted it.
Laughing boys kicked it around.

Up and down the line --
a red skull with hair.

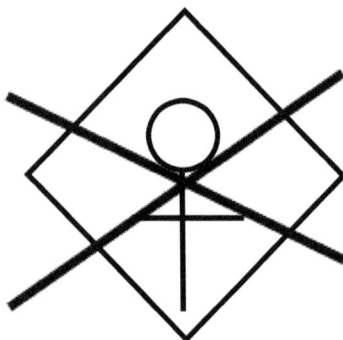

BAGHDAD MURDER: KNEELING MAN

He was shot while kneeling in rocks
by the road.

Hands and elbows bound.
Shoulder blades protruded

like budding wings.

His forehead pressed on the ground
as though at prayer.

Blood discolored the dust.
He offered the perfect curve of his spine

to the sky.

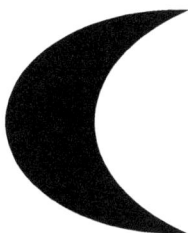

MOSQUE MONITORING

Every Friday we listened at mosques.
A terp recorded sermons.
Afterwards, soldiers worked the crowd.

Who was the speaker?
What did he say?
Where was he from?

Most people walked past, eyes down.
An occasional angry man demanded --
Why are you here?
When will you leave?

Back at headquarters,
the terp sat alone in a small room
with paper and a recorder.

Most weeks he translated messages
calling for the soldiers' deaths
or his.

But tonight he heard
a man weeping, pleading
for God

to stop the teetering world
from toppling on his tiny congregation.
How he pounded his palms and fists
against the iron doors of heaven.

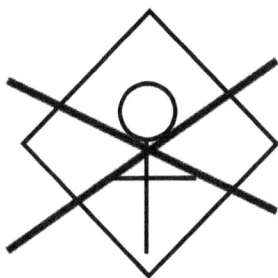

BEHEADING EVENT

Mujahedin gathered the town around
a Shia.
His truck broke down nearby.
He sat bound, blindfolded by the mosque.
Kids and women pointed.
Men chatted, laughed in groups.

Some cursed or spat at him.
Halfhearted, guards restrained them.
A hooded man revved a circular saw.
Applause.
Then he shut it off.
Just a check!

The stranger pleaded -- *My mother
is Sunni. Father once lived
nearby.* Boys approached,

chucked empty water bottles
which collected like
plastic teardrops at his feet.

SEARCH FOR KIDNAPPING
VICTIMS, RADWANIYAH

The soldiers heard reports
of kidnapping victims,
instead found rocks
and a sleeping man
chained to engine blocks.

He'll run off, the uncle sighed.
What would you suggest?

*He used to swear, piss
in the house, growl at the guests.*

*He's slipped off ropes, smashed
bedrooms where he slept.
We built a hut, collared his neck . . .*

Startled awake, he leapt

at the soldiers. Anchored chain

yanked him back. He fell

and whimpered. Men laughed.
Slacking links tinkled -- tiny bells.

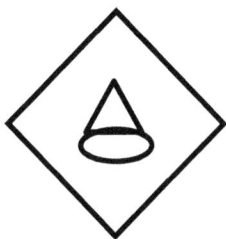

SHIA VENDOR IN SUNNI BAGHDAD

Every day held threats
for him. His emails read
        You're next.
Night letters cradled bullets.
Phone calls, gunshots, texts
with beheading attachments
for months.

His wife was a wreck.

He refused to believe those
he served for years,
winked at their children,
gave each a slice of pear,

wanted him dead.

He refused to hear.

He opened his shop
the morning after
two old friends threaded
trip wire from the threshold of the door

to three mortar rounds
beneath a crate of dates.
His boot heel triggered them.
Blown back fifteen yards,

the blast shredded his shirt.
His one still-attached arm raised
as if greeting a customer.

A smile plain on his face
as neighbors looted the shelves.

They cheered.
Red Crescent
whisked him away.

```
      ╱╲
     ╱  ╲
    ╱    ╲
   ╱      ╲
  ⟨ VBIED ⟩
   ╲      ╱
    ╲    ╱
     ╲  ╱
      ╲╱
```

HOAX

MARKING VBIEDS

Baghdad brothers heard al-Qaeda marked VBIEDs
with X's of tape on car roofs, hoods. Word
got out –
    If you spot one, run away.

Americans found such a sedan,
blew it in place with a water charge.
Doors shot open, trunk spun off,
fluttered like a tossed playing card.

When their physics teacher failed the brothers --
Some BS test --
they found his car that night.

They taped an X on top,
called Terror Tips Line.
Americans came at dawn,
cordoned the street.

Stepping out for work, the teacher pointed -- *That's my car . . .*
From their window the brothers watched.
The teacher yelled -- *It's not a bomb, you idiots!*

The brothers fell from sight
when he screamed

That's my fucking car!!

◇ SAFE ◇

EVERYWHERE THE STARS

Green stars grace Iraqi flags,
aligned with *God is Great*.
Painted flags everywhere –
sidewalks, garage doors, store front signs.

We heard insurgents knew
a building welcomed them if
the stars on the flag looked not green
but blue. We smashed the doors
with sledgehammers. The only problem –

sunlight faded all the stars
to blue. Blue stars on the street
in the windows. Blue stars held
in waving hands. Blue stars

on doors and posters
by the roads. On soccer balls
and passing cars – blue stars, blue
stars, blue stars.

◇ GRENADE ◇

HATRED

Driving through Baghdad that summer,
the soldiers forgot for a moment
where they were, and who--
they lowered their windows.

One hundred yards away
they had to stop –

a herd of goats.

Some guy walked up,

dropped a grenade
in the truck cab,
dismissive as trash.

It thudded
at the TC's feet.
He reached
to toss it out.

It blew
before he threw,
shearing four fingers.

Walking away, the attacker looked back,
smiled and waved.

Inside the truck,
the soldier's rifle lay
smashed.

He thrust
his one
remaining

middle
finger
up.

HELICOPTER FLYOVER, SABA AL-BOOR

Farmers wave.
Three hundred feet
separate us.

So tiny they look
from here,
they could plow our palms,
scale the date palm trunk
of our thumbs.

They urge --
Come here! Come close!

Their mandibles clench
as primal eyes uplift.

HELICOPTER RIDE WITH
CADAVER DOG

It was hot on the chopper.
On top of that,
a cadaver dog sat
big as Sunday
beside me.

He stared out the glass.
His tongue unrolled
like a carpet.
The handler stroked his ear.

Well heeled,
this dog.

I laughed.

What I wouldn't give
for an open window.

The dog leaning into

ninety-knot breeze,
barking.

Barking his fool head off.

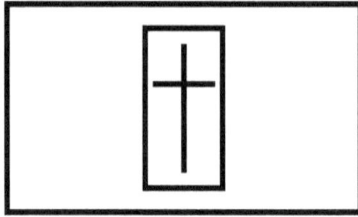

DRAGGING HUSSEIN PALACE RECREATIONAL LAKE FOR BODIES

They're lying in the lake. We dredged up

tires and trash, a crocodile skull.
Not one human bone.

Divers delved the reeds –
seven goats, a deer.

Dig beneath the dates.

We bulldozed his groves –
just roots –
then ripped through the zoo.
Not a femur.

Locals insisted –
Hussein played cards there
on the naked backs of kneeling whores

then locked them with bears.

Sample hair strands in the cage, they urged.
The walls run red when it rains.

IED

FRUIT STAND

It must have seemed funny to the Iraqis.
A convoy hit an IED, a small one --
no one hurt, no damage.
The commander, who literally pissed himself,
hopped out and tottered
to the stand with his terp to ask

who knew anything about it. Out of breath, stuttering,
a frightened Elmer Fudd. It must have seemed funny
because the fruit stand owner laughed
at him as he spoke. The customers
laughed. Women and children
laughed. First snickers and giggles then

unhideable guffaws. Finger-pointing,
head-shaking, tear-drawing
laughter. Laughter escorting the commander
back to his truck where he retrieved
from the trunk a baseball bat and two SAW gunners.
The laughter quieted.

The customers stepped back
and the store owner ducked
as the commander suddenly swung his bat
into the melons, dates, soda cans,
water bottles, oranges.
Now laughter perked up from the Humvees,

the guards, the commander screaming,
Who's laughing now,
as his pulp-dripping bat rose and fell.

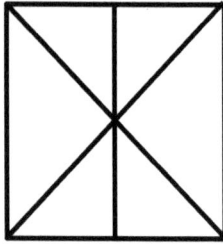

IRAQI ARMY UNIT ON CAMP
STRIKER

Their colonel met our colonel inside
the TOC to build
    a partnership.
His troops waited outside,
lit fires by their Humvees,
cooked chow and laughed.
Sparks swirled as if they conjured a genie.

They acted like they never used
a porta-john before.
Each Soldier filed in twice,
emerged doubled
with guffaws.

They doused their heads with Aquafina,
dumped water cans of *Ma-a*
on the embers,
settled down to snore
splayed across the hoods.

Their colonel returned at midnight,
motioned.

The soldiers scurried,
Humvees coughed,
pulled out
and left behind

black ash pits and packs
of empty MRE Halal,
crushed water bottles

and in the latrines

fecal graffiti –

FUCK U.S.
AND ALL UR MOTHERS!

CHRISTMAS EVE NIGHT ON AN IRAQI PZ, 2004

Christmas Eve 1968, I mistook aircraft lights
for reindeer.

Tonight, sky-hooves
churn darkness to chaff.

Through the blast of their settling
we clamber the frames,
buck from the earth

leaving four dented coke cans,
three candy wrappers,
two plastic bottles,
and a tan, empty MRE sack
to drape on a tree as we rise.

44

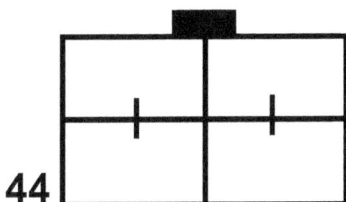

44TH FIELD HOSPITAL,
CHRISTMAS, 2003

On Christmas I visited
some local patients, amputees or burned.
A little boy cried as I entered,
wiggling his stumped and bandaged arms.

Other patients greeted me
or turned their heads away--
teens and three old men, a set of twins
who played hot potato with a hand grenade.

Salaam, Khef al-halak? I asked.
"OK. Hello!" the twins replied in perfect English.
I had matching socks
for them, thick and wool,
and stocking caps for everybody else.

The unconscious, the sleeping,
the dying, I placed the gifts at their feet.

As I left, an orderly
swirled a grey mop over my boot prints.

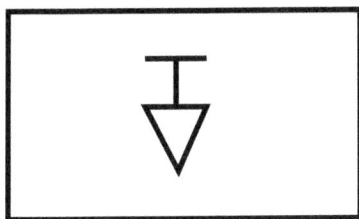

KINGS

It's good to be kings.
We're winning the war,
ruling the world.

We enter a dining hall.
Ugandan guards check our I.D.s.
Their English is perfect.
They have degrees,
fathers with connections.
In Uganda, this is *punk work.*
Here, it's crazy money.

Bangladeshis serve pork chops,
mop our spills, heave trash.
More rice, sir?
They dream periodic tables,
wipe Formica white.

In their lands
these men are sons of privilege, kings.
Here, issued hairnet crowns,

their scepters metal ladles,
bomb detection wands.

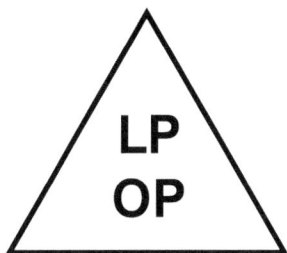

PUPPIES

His mother sneered *When puppies fly*
instead of *No.* He imagined
they could

flap huge ears, extend their legs,
arf like gulls above.
Mother

repeated that mocking phrase
when he joined the Army.
Now look! Iraq!

A stray litter suckled near the CP --
trembling mascots. That night
he snuck

them up a guard tower in wriggling
bags. He unwrapped them
like jewels,

stroked and kissed each nose before he
launched them star-ward
laughing.

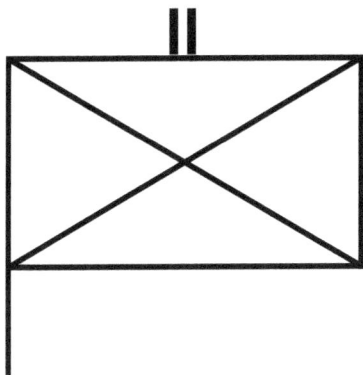

NIGHT DUST STORM AND SOLDIERS WITH LASER POINTERS, JOINT SECURITY STATION LOYALTY, BAGHDAD, IRAQ

They illumine passing particles,
transform to Jedi Knights.

Green and scarlet sabers
sweep like spotlights
marking cinema, car sale.

Dust is diced by curve and slice
of light thin as guitar strings.

They clash until batteries die,
bow, christen each other

Obi Wan and *Darth* --

sheathe swords in pockets,
hilts warm with grip and palm.

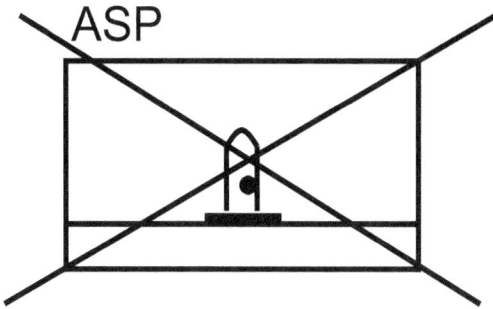

BURNING AMMUNITION
SUPPLY POINT

We watched it on our camera in the TOC.
Beyond the hill blasts crested -- a series of sunrises.

Someone flipped on CNN. They broadcasted
what we saw –
fists of fire thrusting.
The exact same scene.

A sergeant thought they had our feed,
told a soldier to pan
to a chicken coop
just outside the camp.
See if CNN moves.
Of course, nothing changed.

But on our screen
a boy pointed. A man

with a hand on his head
turned to hush his hens
fluttering in the rising, falling
half light of the flames.

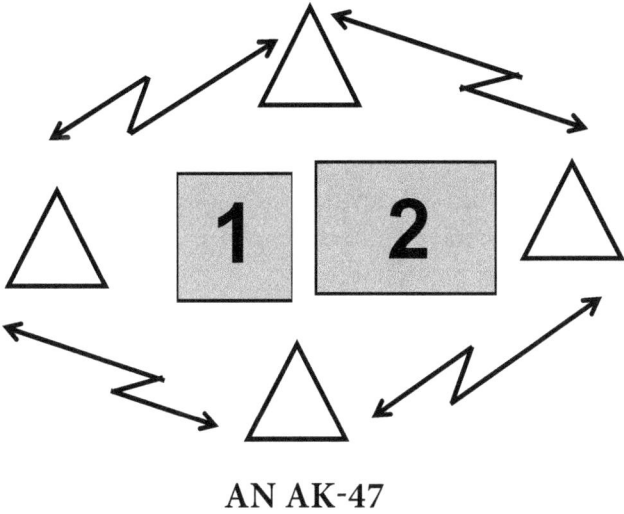

AN AK-47

Americans knocked one day at a house. They heard
the man stored guns
crated, clean and oiled.

> *He's a big-shot in JAM!*

The man followed the soldiers,
opening doors, pointing, explaining.
A squad of children tagged behind.

> *Neighbors hate me. I'm Shia.*
> *They'll say anything to drive me out.*

He shook his head.

The search dogs found
one AK-47 hanging on two hooks
above the front doorframe,
clip inserted in the well.

The man pulled it down,
cleared it, showed it to the captain.
The captain handed it back
and asked,

Why hang it on the wall?

The man turned left and right,
extended one hand toward six boys
who stretched as one to touch
the cradled rifle.

Detainee
Holding
Area

EXCEL SPREADSHEET --
DETAINEE RELEASE LIST

It's numbing
         how uniform
         1,000 men appear
listed on a spreadsheet --
         cities, dates,
         numbers and times
lined straight
         as the sandbags
         of a bunker.
Their names melt
         into a sticky
         confluence --
AbdarrahimSahimIbrahimSadounSalmanAswad
    AbuQays
         It's hard to discern
         whose beaming families,
weeping mothers, are whose
         gathered at the prison gates.
         It's hard not to feel
happy for them:
         humans,
         not text,
wrapping around.

APOE

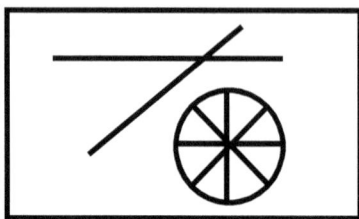

BAGHDAD INTERNATIONAL AIRPORT, AS VIEWED FROM CAMP STRIKER, IRAQ

As a boy, we passed an airport
en route to the beach --

crop dusters lined the grass beside
wingless DC-3s,
a tri-tailed Constellation
minus engines and nosecone.

Hooded Pipers
still as pastured colts.

Stationed near BIAP,
I glanced daily
at a distant grounded IraqAir jumbo jet.
It never budged.

Indifferent
to the world's dark swirlings,
the mortars and rocket plumes
forming nearby cumulus.

A being,
a thing unmoved,
this plane,

decidedly
at rest.

APOE

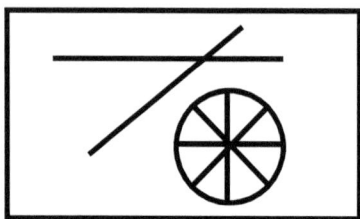

MY LAST DAY IN BAGHDAD

I spent it at the airport
amid the mega-fan sound of propellers,
drawn-out wheeze of jets.

Above the din
a kilometer south or so,
three mortar rounds exploded, or maybe

a car bomb, RPGs.
Who knew? I didn't.
I didn't turn my head.

My plane sidled up.
I filed to the stairs.
Boarding, I noticed

a black plume of smoke
wave slowly as if

in the distant fist
of a well wisher.

REFERENCES: ALL REFERENCES AND DEFINITIONS DERIVE FROM FIELD MANUAL (FM) 101-5-1, 30 SEP 97, UNLESS OTHERWISE INDICATED.

APOD

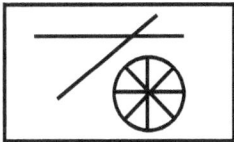

Air Point of Debarkation (APOD) (Friendly): the geographic point in a routing scheme from which cargo or personnel depart. (pp. 1-122, figure, 4-29)

APOE

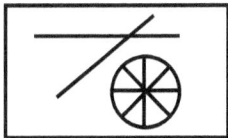

Air Point of Embarkation (APOE) (Friendly): the geographic point in a routing scheme from which cargo or personnel embark. (pp. 1-122, figure, 4-29)

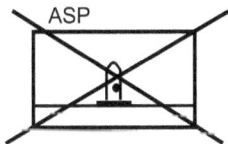

ASP

Ammunition Supply Point (Friendly) destroyed. (figure, 4-28)

Aviation Axis of Advance (Friendly): A general route of advance, assigned for purposes of control, which extends toward the enemy. (pp. 1-14, figure, 3-14)

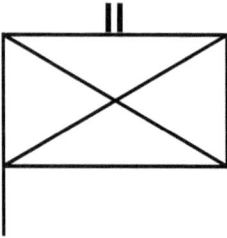

Battalion Headquarters (Infantry) (Friendly): (figure, 4-5

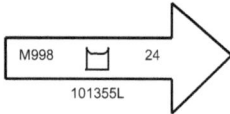

Convoy: A group of vehicles that moves over the same route at the same time and under one commander. (pp. 1-39, figure, 3-37)

Convoy, halted. (figure, 3-37)

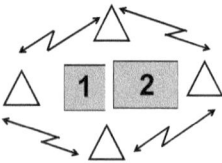

Cordon and search (or knock). (figure, modified)

Detained person during friendly operations. (figure, modified)

Detainee: A term used to refer to any person captured or otherwise detained by an armed force. (pp. 1-52, figure, 3-37)

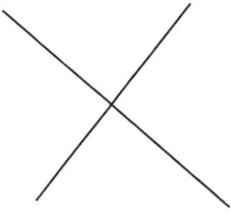

Destroy: 1. A tactical task to physically render an enemy force combat ineffective unless it is reconstituted. 2. To render a target so damaged that it cannot function as intended nor be restored to a usable condition without being entirely rebuilt. (pp. 1-51, figure, C-9)

Enemy use of booby trap. (figure, D-3)

Enemy use of graffiti. (figure, D-4)

Enemy use of grenade. (figure, modified)

Enemy use of improvised explosive device (IED). (figure, modified)

Enemy use of kidnapping. (figure D-5)

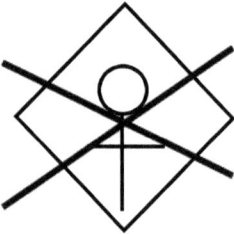

Enemy use of murder or killing of a civilian. (figure, D-3, modified)

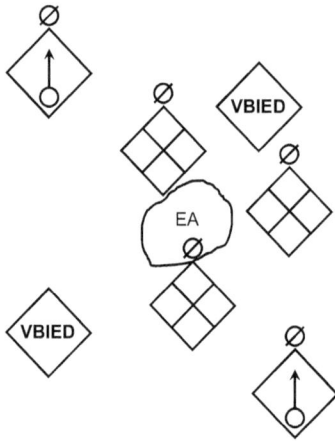

Enemy use of raid: An operation, usually small scale, involving a swift penetration of hostile territory to secure information, confuse the enemy, or to destroy installations. It ends with a planned withdrawal upon completion of the assigned mission. Above is depicted a very basic example of a raid, involving enemy mortars, VBIEDs and infantry arrayed to strike an engagement area (EA). (pp. 1-127, figure, example)

Enemy use of safe house: An innocent-appearing house or premises established by an organization for the purpose of conducting clandestine or covert activity in relative security. (pp. 1-136, figure, D-7)

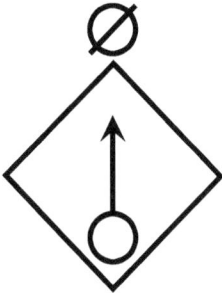

Enemy use of 60mm Mortar Team. (figure, 5-8)

Enemy use of suicide vest IED, or SVIED. (figure, modified)

Enemy use of vehicle-borne IED, or VBIED. (figure, modified)

Enemy use of VBIED hoax, often emplaced to distract American forces. (definition mine) (figure, modified)

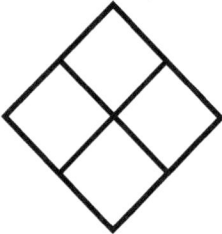

Hostile or insurgent infantry. (figure, D-5)

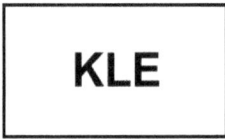

Key Leader Engagement (Friendly): Meeting between US troops and leading local representatives to foster cooperation or understanding between the two groups. (definition mine, figure, modified)

Labor (Friendly). (figure, 4-25)

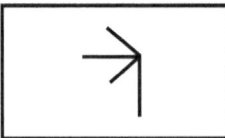

Laundry and Bath (Friendly). (figure, 4-25, modified)

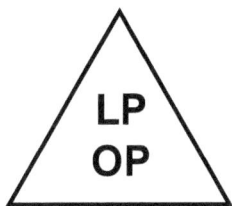

Listening post/observation post: A position from which military observations are made, or fire directed and adjusted, and which possesses appropriate communications. (pp. 1-112, figure, 4-17, modified)

Living Support Area, normally barracks or sleep areas (Friendly). (definition mine) (figure, modified)

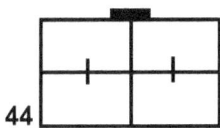

Medical Treatment Facility (Friendly): A facility established for the purpose of furnishing medical and/or dental care to eligible individuals. (pp. 1-99, figure, 4-26)

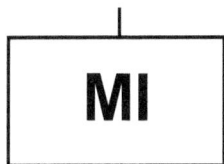

Military Intelligence Company (Friendly). (figure, 4-19)

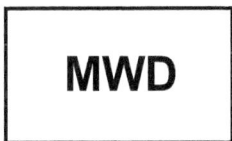

Military Working Dogs, AKA bomb-sniffing or cadaver - seeking dogs (Friendly). (definition mine) (figure, modified)

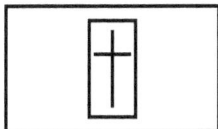

Mortuary affairs (Friendly): Broadly based military program to provide care and disposition of deceased personnel. (pp. 1-105, figure, 4-26)

Mosque. (figure, modified)

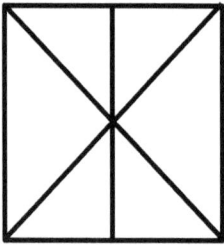

Motorized Infantry (Iraqi or Neutral). (figure, 4-17, modified)

Pickup Zone (PZ): A geographic area used to pick up troops or equipment by helicopter. (pp. 1-121, figure, 3-13)

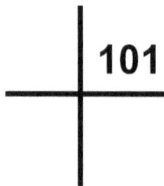

Target Reference Point (TRP): An easily recognizable point on the ground (either natural or manmade) used to initiate, distribute, and control fires. (pp. 1-152, figure, 3-9)

SP

Start Point: A well-defined point on a route at which a movement of vehicles begins to be under the control of the commander of this movement. It is at this point that the column is formed by the successive passing, at an appointed time, of each of the elements composing the column. (pp. 1-144, figure, 3-26)

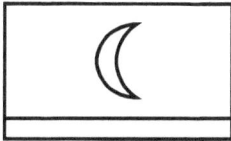

Supply class I (Friendly), subsistence (food and water). (pp. 1-27, figure, 4-27)

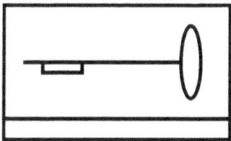

Supply Class II (Friendly), clothing, individual equipment, etc. (pp. 1-27, figure, 4-28)

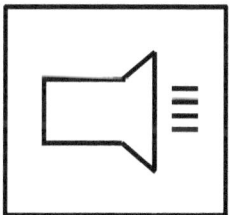

Psychological Operations (Iraqi or Neutral): Planned operations to convey selected information and indicators to foreign audiences their emotions, motives, objective reasoning, and ultimately the behavior of foreign governments, organizations, groups, and individuals. The purpose of psychological operations is to induce or reinforce foreign attitudes and behavior favorable to the originator's objectives. (pp. 1-125, figure, 4-30, modified)

DISPATCHES FROM THE FOB

ANTHOLOGY POEMS

Contents

INTRODUCTION

Each soldier's wartime deployment in Iraq and Afghanistan produced different experiences. For me, I existed in two disparate spheres: the operational and the literary. On the operational side, every work day (12 to 20 hours), I examined documents, analyzed and composed reports, studied events of varying brutality, ferocity, and lethality. Some days, I heard explosions. Some days, those explosions were close. On the literary side, if I possessed the energy, I would retreat to my sleep area and read the poetry collections which accompanied me to the Middle East. Some of them further unsettled me, while others bolstered my will to fulfill the duties I had to complete, and fly home to my family.

When I returned to the United States, I felt compelled to contemplate and record both the mundane and inhumane acts I understood, found in *FM 101-5-1 Operational Terms and Graphics*, incorporated into the kaleidoscopic mosaic of "me." Poetry, that literary sphere, transformed from a source of figurative sustenance to one of physical criticality, a cornea through which I viewed what I saw and knew to exist in the operational arena. The authors within *Flying Over Baghdad With Sylvia Plath: Experiences, Through Poetry, with Poets and Poems in Iraq and Afghanistan*, and many others who bravely faced their own experiences (Allison Pitinii Davis, Claudia Cortese, and

Susan Harper Slaviero, for example) encouraged me to explore, sift, and excavate the blur of 2002-2010 in the solitude and reflection great literature provides.

I incorporated these two collections and included additional poems which I believe help serve a bridge between the two books. In the end, my experiences forced these disparate universes, operational and literary, to coexist. I found the world to be hard, but livable. And I found these writers living in the same, hard world, lifting to their mouths scraps of meat pulled straight from the fires of their own making.

BAGHDAD MURDER: MIDDLE-AGED MARRIED COUPLE

Together forever
we would sigh
if it were romantic

for thugs to bind them
back-to-back
with duct tape,
their gag adhesive wrap.

The world burns around them.

There is no sweetness in a city
warring itself.

There cannot be love.

Is this why it is stupid to think
the couple now laughs together

as if they left a party
arm-in-arm, music muffled
as they strolled?

Isn't it enough
they strained
to touch?

Their stroking thumbs
sufficed.

PETS

In Iraq, death always
had its way.

When I came home,
my fish's fins rotted.

The bunny blotched
with tumors.

I bought ten-dollar medicine drops
for the two-dollar barb.

The vet nodded, stroking the rabbit.
I would pay
the five hundred bucks.

Death could not just visit
my house
any time it felt like
filling its black palms.

THE MOUSE IN IRAQ

The corner of the eye revealed a flash of gray
and fluff. A flit across the floor
and a stapler bounced beside it
or someone threw a book, and the mouse
slipped beneath a tent wall into the night.

Night after night we schemed its death—
the traps and poison, the wistful hope
it would bite a wire down to the copper current.

One soldier among us prayed
we'd fail to kill it, shooed it safely
from our sight, crumbled a cracker
in the corner mixed with jam.

The same soldier who saw the enemy
as people, not deserving death or detention,
not deserving the fire of their own devices.
Both men and mice, she thought, should live
even in the dark. Someone with the power
to kill them should relent, bring others
to relenting.

HOMECOMING WITH YOUNG CHILDREN

My son bounces,
a frantic puppy.
My daughter stands
on my feet, demands --
Walk, Daddy!

Let the teen carry bags!

My wife can ride shotgun,
teenager drive.

I sit in the back.
There's no resisting.

At home, hardwood shines
like the surface of a pool.
We dive in.
The world's roughest
tickle fight!

Roaring and shouts.
Our collie exhausts herself
barking.

My kids have learned
to play it tougher,
tag team up.

They don't know their strength

with their kicks to the spine,
fists to the chest,
laughs all the way
to the bone.

THE MORTIS DOGS

Every other night I dreamed
of dogs,

not
the puppies which nuzzled my chin,
gobbled beneath my table
each length of wheat bread crust
I hid from Mom,
then slipped
at the feet of the dining room chair.

Not them.

I dreamed
of mortis dogs,
mongrels
stalking Baghdad.

In my sleep they slinked,
their flanks black
as burned Humvees,
eyes bone white.
Their incisors
red with rat meat.
Fresh scabs oozed green pus.

Lords of the trash piles,
their heavy paws
dwarfed our boot prints.

Mortis dogs, the ones
which did not
bark or
tuck their tails,
or cower when we passed
in our thunderous Strykers,

but stared instead
and panted, grinning
and waiting
for the IED blast

to draw them like a whistle
to our bleeding sides,
to lick us clean

without malice,
without love,

then sniff from us our breath
and escort us
when we rose

to their master.

FOB HAMMER'S MINI-CHRISTMAS TREES, 2009

That December, a stateside nursery boxed and shipped
five hundred live, fresh
tiny Christmas trees,

complete with ornaments and hooks,
to grace dusty FOB Hammer,
officially listed in The World Book Almanac as

The Place You Are Least Likely
to Find a Live Christmas Tree.

In every office the scent of pine.
Needles sprinkled the desks.

Glass Santas and pinecones
dangled from the limbs.

Soldiers hung chem-lites Christmas Eve
to glow above their packages
of corn nuts.

On New Year's Day, I passed a dumpster.
Twenty mini-spruces jutted amid the plastic bags
and water bottles,
soda cans and MREs.

That night I pulled them out,
lugged them half a mile
to thrust them upright in a dune
behind the motor pool.

I heaved a case of water there
and poured

every night I could,
though I knew one day we'd leave
and the trees would die,

and the glass snowmen,
candy canes remaining
would twist like the condemned
amid the shreds of tinsel

and brown needles
un-knitting the trees.

CELLPHONES

The owners?
Killed in a raid
that night.

We grabbed their phones,
zipped them in plastic,
threw them
in the Humvee.

Time passed.

Suddenly,
a call,

the ringtone
Jump Around!

The phones glowed green.

By nine AM,
they chirped
nonstop –

caged birds
in an empty store.

AFTER RETURNING FROM THE WAR, I LISTEN TO A YOUTUBE CLIP OF LIBERTYCHICKLIVE

Hearing her, I wonder if there's blood now sticking
even to my keys as I type and recall
the war in which
I was either

    . . . dumb, evil, or morally compromised.

Tacky blood

which makes even shifting
my fingers beyond
the home keys hard.

    Many people in the military,
    they don't actually
    know . . .

I passed off
data to commanders:
family, address, car.

    what they're doing.

I clicked coordinates
to pilots in Nevada
unleashing their Hellfires.

They think

Rubbing my palms, there is
only
the sweat of a glass, of a brow.

      that they're helping
      us, that they're

My pinkies are clean
as the surface
of an ice cube, quick

as it slides
across Formica.

      protecting their country.

I don't want to
write about the war
anyway, or

read up
on The Sunni Triangle,
Shia ethnic cleansing in Hurriyah.
I want

      a valid excuse

to teach my son how
to send a note
in invisible ink.

Dip a Q-Tip in lemon juice,
draw your name on notebook paper, say
how much
I love my daddy!

Hold the sheet above
a bare bulb,

      Ignorance isn't going to

discern the letters rising
slow as the shoots of tulip bulbs
buried in the fall.

Milk works just as well.
Both hold
sufficient acid.

My son folds a note to Mom,
dysgraphic Rs and Ns.

      The sheet must be dry
      for letters to appear.

      To me, that's disgusting

We lift the shade
of a table lamp.

It flings its 60 watts of bald light
across the living room
like a super ball.

The easy chair casts
invective shadow
up the wall.

        I'm not
        gonna help you out

The message is clear. Mom
reads the sweetness, smiles.
But by then

we're bored with letters,
juice, and Q-Tips.
I show my boy a trick.

        It's not gonna change

I tell him to shutter his eyes
with his fingers, so tight
no light
leaks through,
then face
the naked bulb

        the Iraqi people.

Do you see the red?
Did you know
it's blood?

Did you know that much
blood flows through

a human hand?

    And I
    believe that.

ACKNOWLEDGEMENTS

"After Returning from the War, I Listen to a YouTube clip of LibertyChickLive," *Red Earth Review*

"Baghdad Murder: Middle-Aged Married Couple," *Provo Canyon Review*

"Cellphones," *Licking River Review*

"FOB Hammer's Mini-Christmas Trees, 2009," *Hobble Creek Review*

"Pets," *UCity Review*

"The Mortis Dogs," *District Lit*

"The Mouse in Iraq," *Crab Creek Review*

FLYING OVER BAGHDAD WITH SYLVIA PLATH

EXPERIENCES, THROUGH POETRY, WITH POETS AND POEMS IN IRAQ AND AFGHANISTAN

"I don't want poetry to limit itself to reflecting or recapitulating experience;

I want it to
be
an experience."

-- Lisa Olstein

Contents

INTRODUCTION

Poetry as hero, not heroic poetry. Just masterful verse which performs extraordinary work in extraordinary circumstances. No one has, likely, ever uttered the words, "Read Jennifer Kronovet's collection; it will save your life!" That is, until today.

Because it has, for me. All the poets introduced here have literally plucked me from flames. I had to make sense of Afghanistan, Iraq, The Surge, our Senate's approval of The Surge, my family's struggles in my absence, and the moral decrepitude of the undertakings of conflict, these ones, and all the ones before.

Years ago, poet Donald Finkel introduced me to the writings of Albert Goldbarth. His piece "Knees/ Dura-Europos" made me grasp the overwhelming continuity of war, its timelessness, and how Goldbarth confronted it with lines like, "This is what's happening now," and, "This is what's going to happen." So, the question is, What is poetry doing about it? Because we know war happened, happens, and will happen again.

Well, if you ask the poets represented in this book, they can truly say, "We are denying it an enclave;" "We have named it what it is;" "We have plowed its fields with salt;" "We have refused to clothe or feed it." There is no need to charge barricades. These poets have denied war the ability to traverse their land, in the time-honored guerilla fashion of refusing an enemy sustenance, support, a base from which to operate and raze surrounding country. While I served in President Bush's wars, their work became a series of safe houses, places I could find sympathy and support.

So now, having departed these conflicts, reviewing my experiences, I pin these tiny medals on the poets who did a hero's work, pulled me from the fire, fed me bread and wine in the dark, warm corners of their books.

SUSAN HAHN WROTE A POEM ABOUT HARRIET RUBIN'S MOTHER'S WOODEN HAND

I knew I had to write about the war
the moment I read Hahn's poem --

how she balanced
the world
on the apex
of Mrs. Rubin's juniper knuckle.

I wanted to perch
all I was worth
on the rickety wagon an Afghan toddler pulled
with four upright five-gallon jugs
filled to spilling
uphill.

I had to remember
the bass drum pound
of the outgoing round,

concussive gut-suck
of the incoming one-oh-seven.

Even in summer Chicago
Mrs. Rubin sported gloves.

At home, I shrugged on sweaters in June,
slipped a North Face fleece
in the back of my Saturn
year round.

I needed to
never forget the Iraqi translator
who daily donned black
because cousins and nephews were dying

so fast,

she never managed
to shed her mourning abaya.

I had to understand why
I slumped
stuffed like ten pounds of shit
in a five pound bag,

why children
on Mrs. Rubin's block
snickered when she passed,

and recoiled
at the apple she offered
with her one good hand.

A SOLDIER LOANS ME HER COPY OF SYLVIA PLATH'S *THE COLLECTED POEMS*

When she heard I loved poetry,
she handed me her copy.
That volume I had chosen
not to bring from home
pursued me like a Fate.

I had hoped that year not to hear
"Daddy" and "The Applicant."

    Your head, excuse me, is empty

Now she would fill it with her teacups,
as her pinkie hooked my belt loop.

    Come here, sweetie

In this land of match sticks and flint,

    I made a fire, being tired

she swept her hand across its rough surface
and laughed.

    Do I terrify?

What could I do

but open the door to my CHU
and throw her on the bed,
throw myself.

She sang with the springs
as she opened

    Love, love, my season.

ROMANCING CHRISTINE GARREN'S *AMONG THE MONARCHS* DESPITE CENTRAL COMMAND'S GENERAL ORDER 1

The order states No Drinking No Drugs No
Gambling No Converting the Afghans to Christ

No Bringing a Girl to your Room No Mailing Home
a Weapon or Live Spiders No Sex with Anyone
not Your Wife No Destroying or Stealing
National Treasures

Polled, you answer

Yes Yes No Yes
Yes Definitely No Maybe No

It's hard
to figure you out.

When I set you on the bed and pull
you close,
you sigh
>   *Now no one is here. Not even I am here*
>   *in full.*

You in your white gown,
necklace of onyx,
obsidian earrings.

My calloused fingers catch on the saffron.
You unhook and set
those useless tools aside.

But I want,
I want to get in,

resort to fingering
the bone of your wrist.

Maybe there is
as you say

a door there,
a knob, when touched just so,
which turns.

FINDING WHAT IN RACHEL CONTRENI FLYNN'S *ICE, MOUTH, SONG* BRINGS ME TO CONCLUDE IT IS ORACULAR

I talk to God. Sometimes
He is silent
when I ask

-- Why did we find a child hanging
from a ceiling fan in Baghdad,
his murdered family lying neatly
beneath his sweeping shadow?

-- Why am I falling apart?

I opened her book.
> *Our father . . .*
> *the flat stone of himself . . .*

And it spoke to me.

My mother was committed to an asylum
while I was deployed.

When I read "State Home, 1984,"
I found comfort in the grapefruit's
> *happy eye.*

After I spoke with her on the phone
I read "The Trap,"
unfurled, displayed my little flags.

These were not
the only mysteries she solved.

               At dusk,
     deer with well-hidden zippers advance.
I scanned the walls from my watch tower,
a little more tense that night.

She asked
          Is this my mother or a sad tablet?

I took the chance
and tossed my Paxil.

When she sang
          I will not be sad
I considered it.

I studied her poems
as some read tea leaves
swirled and dumped
in the dip of a saucer.

The black on white arrangement
which
to unbelievers
seemed
like gibberish,

those dregs on the porcelain dish

slipping this way and that.

KATHLEEN GRABER'S *CORRESPONDENCE* GIVES ME A PAPER CUT AFTER A HARD DAY IN IRAQ

Blood for oil, I muse
as the tiny rivulet creasing the print of my thumb
fills like a stream in the spring
to overflowing.

I get
this is no injury,
no Purple Heart forthcoming,
no lauding from the colonel
as the medal's honed pin passes
a half-inch from my skin.

We were talking
about distance, how unimaginably far
between the stars, even planets.
Who could bridge them?
Who could dip their oars and row
a million, billion years?

And now this stupid cut
distracts us from "The Letters,"
"The Language of Bees."
A slender stain soaks the edge
of "Terra Incognita."

Does it sting?

-- You bet your ass.

We're tight like that.

She knows that men are dying.
My cut merits
not even half a caesura
in the war's least readable history.

It doesn't stop her --
Blood for oil, she laughs.

An oil that fouls and cakes
within a minute in the air.

No wonder, she notes,
war's cylinders need
so often to be lathed and bored.

AT THE END OF THE DAY, I GET CREEPED OUT BY LOUISE GLUCK'S DETACHED TONE IN *ARARAT*

A pilot on doom's precipice
transmitting calmly –
Tower, we are going down

has nothing on her lines –
> *She wants to be back in the cemetery,*
> *back in the sickroom, the hospital.*

All day I read of death
in reports
written in the manner
of a nurse who has seen

herself the cancerous lesions, traumatic
amputation of the lower right leg below the knee,
anaphylactic reaction to shellfish.

Gluck's lyrics are clean
as the mirrored
steel
of scalpels,
a gleaming tray of them
set beside
the anesthetized patient.

The masked surgeon
betrays nothing
as she lifts a blade
and slits the pallid flesh beneath
to flowering.

WHAT WAS I THINKING, BRINGING ADRIENNE RICH'S *A WILD PATIENCE HAS TAKEN ME THIS FAR?*

A car needs brakes. A rifle, a safety switch.
And where I was going, who knew
what I would see or need

to survive?

We were taught to plan
for any eventuality.

The army even issued
a seatbelt cutter
to each Soldier in case
the truck around her burned.

Our uniforms were fireproof.
Our body armor plates could stop a bullet
dead.

I should have known better

than to uncork those pages
in my dark room after work,
the flashlight's white finger
quaking.

Each night I
conjured the ghost of Ethel Rosenberg
trapped within the book.

Each night
I dove into the wreck

of my life,

she filled the room
with her boxcutter tongue,

jabbed in my face
the bayonet point of her nail.

Stupid fuck, she sneered.

You stupid, stupid fuck.

YUSUF KOMUNYAKAA'S BOOK *DIEN CAI DAU* ASSUMES THE ROLE OF COMMISERATING OLD SOLDIER

I need to talk.

Of course.

Who else will listen?

No one else.

Well, I woke one night to a mortar
whistling low as a strolling beat cop.

    this one died looking up at the sky

That one didn't even see the trip wire.

    What made me spot the monarch
    writhing on a single thread

I don't know,
but I sure am glad.

A rocket blew out my window once

    Like a benediction of blue

Exactly!

Where you would have been that moment

but I stopped to take a leak.

What did I know about war?

I feel like I'm down there

Why did I talk
to the recruiter like she was a girl lounging
on a beach?

a flash of legs

And I wrenched
my shirt off and sprinted with her
        into the whitecaps,
        laughing.

WHY DID I E-MAIL SUSAN MCCASLIN TO PURCHASE *FLYING WOUNDED* WHILE SERVING IN IRAQ?

I don't know.

I'm not sure what I knew
when I asked to buy
her book firsthand.

I don't know why
I contacted a stranger.
A Canadian stranger.

A survivor can't explain
why he turned his car
left instead of right,
and the bridge he crossed each day
collapsed in his rearview mirror.

The book addressed her mother,
not the war.
Looking back,

I was cracking.

I was tapping
my S.O.S. on the pipes,

transmitting into empty space
and listening,
listening

for that tiny tick
on the teletype,

deciphering a dot or dash
within the static fields,

or a voice atop the ruins
and the rubble being lifted,

dust motes teeming
on the lowering ropes of light.

LISTENING TO KRISTIN HERSH'S SONG "IN SHOCK" WHILE LIVING ON CAMP VICTORY, BAGHDAD, IRAQ

That night, the laptop flickered.
I snapped off every light.

In the darkest room

I held out my hands.
Letters skittered and sniffed –

mice
across the screen.

I clambered Youtube,
knocked on the door
of her song,

stepped in.

where the music's loud

In the next CHU a Soldier was doing
the German laundry girl,
that unmistakable drumming
of bedpost and flesh.

The mouth you're seeking

I turned the music up,
gave up
and got some air.

finds your mouth

I let it play
to soak the space
like Listerine.

Heat pressed my face
with a freshly dried towel.

In shock

Dust sashayed up
stairs of nearby light,
shimmied like
Rihanna
down.

little green apples falling

The music was reduced
to drumbeat.

around you

Between the beats,
I could not

hear the strings,
the hooks,
the chords.

I filled those gaps with lyrics.

I crossed her bridges humming.

CHRISTIANNE BALK AND I DISCUSS SNIPE HUNTING WHILE READING *BINDWEED*

It's one of those talks that go nowhere,
a goose chase of a talk
so late at night the stars have drifted
beyond the light of their lanterns.

I never knew a snipe existed, though you swear
your poem is proof --
  snipe-punctured mud shoals . . .
you wrote.

I've seen them,
you insist.

That's not proof.

You draw me a bird on a napkin,
a fat sandpiper
or maybe a hunchbacked crow.

I snuck new kids at night
to hunt snipe in the woods
deep as the center of a tootsie pop.

Back in ten minutes, I promised,
snickered, disappeared.

They returned next morning
scratched as cat-raked pigeons,
swearing.

They had to break through
the black brush like bulls.
They had to listen for cars.

We don't even talk about loss tonight,
though that's what your book is about.

We don't want to touch
on your dead husband,
my sick wife lying
two oceans away
on a hospital gurney.

What can we say?
There's enough grief on any night
to lose ourselves in,

enough nights to wander
through bindweed and chiggers,

snipes above us on the dark branches
clucking like hens in their sleep.

LYNDA HULL RAISES *GHOST MONEY* TO HAUNT ME OVER THERE

The book cover is purple, in Japan the color
of death.

In the West at worst
a clot, a bruise.
I left
my copy sunk between
Ann Hudson and June Jordan.

In Baghdad, I researched the influences
of the Iraqi Communist Party,
recalled her poem "1933," those lines

    he turns his gentle hand --
after her grandfather meets the doomed Trotsky --
    against himself.

My uncle piloted an LCP
to Omaha Beach in 1944,

my only tenuous link to that war
his sweat and fear,
the men
his boat disgorged
cut down
in the whipsaw crossfire.

And later when Hull's speaker

    watched the police
    drag the river for a suicide,

she couldn't turn away

though the week before I left for war
I had to shove
adrift my father in his bier of satin and aluminum.

I couldn't bear
to touch his stiff, ringed fingers

the shape and hardness of hooks
combing the dark, spongy bottom of a lake
to snag and raise a body
chained and heavy with weeds.

PSYCHOANALYZING A COPY OF LAURA GILPIN'S *HOCUS POCUS OF THE UNIVERSE*, WHICH I BOUGHT AT A LIBRARY SALE

You should have been a movie.
You're that good.
I don't see, either, why
anyone would sell you for a nickel.

Now, it says in your records
you were checked out six times
in thirty years. Please
elaborate.

Three high-school girls took me home
to write reports entitled
"Shifting Perspectives Found in 'The Two-Headed Calf.'"

It sounds like an assignment.

It was. They could have written about anything.

It's a beautiful poem.

Not the only poem.

You're very successful!

A Walt Whitman Prize winner.

It's a major award.

My favorite was "Seeing a Dog in the Rain."
A movie? Do you think?

There's a clip on Youtube about you.
Laura Treacy Bentley reads a poem of yours
in a garden
by a stream.

Let me guess. "The Two-Headed Calf."

Laura,

it's a beautiful,
beautiful poem.

I GET MY MESSIAH COMPLEX ON WITH A COPY OF CYNTHIA ZARIN'S *FIRE LYRIC*

Someone raided a Borders bargain table,
boxed and mailed to soldiers
150 Ways to Lose Weight and Keep it Off,
Successful Business Strategies of William Gates
and *How to Find the Right Guy and Make Him Yours.*

They went straight to our rec room shelves
with Zane Gray novels
and *The Life You Imagine*, by Derek Jeter, with Jack
    Curry.

Let the Iraqis spoon through
Chicken Soup for the Teenage Girl's Soul.

I found huddled at the bottom
of the box, Zarin's *Fire Lyric*
marked down to $3.99.

I grabbed her like an orphan,
pulled her from her cardboard room
and all but ran her home.

She sat tightlipped in the CHU.

She didn't consider herself worthy
of life beyond a box and garbage bin.

She lay for an hour on the bed,
listened as the a/c hummed
like a contented mother
ironing a dress.

She spied forty poets on the shelf
leaning and twittering, glancing her way.

She opened up
and sang

>   *White had a claim upon my heart*

>   *Who doesn't come through the door*
>   *to get home?*

THE COMMANDING PRESENCE
OF KAREN FISH'S
THE CEDAR CANOE

She doesn't look like much: a slim peach
            -- slip of a book.
Is there an ounce
of fat on her bones?

But crack her once,
she'll open a can of whupp-ass.

Whatever she says,   goes.

Though she may be cool as precious metal,
you will do what
she commands.

She points at your chest with five
extended fingers and a flexed forearm.

You'd better listen up
when she issues her orders.

On the shelf, she stands straight as the chimney
of a house burned down.

There's not one soft edge
even when she's as open
as a map.

When she observes
        the water isn't deep
and points out danger zones
        The dirt road that runs down the hill
            -- her dust jacket gleams like polished boots.
Her pages are creased sharp
as the starched sleeves of First Sergeant.

JILLY DYBKA SENDS ME THE DIRT ON BASEBALLS INSIDE A COPY OF *TROUBLE AND HONEY*

The poetry, yeah, poetry.
But what intrigues me is the dirt she sends
on baseballs.

A tiny packet tucked inside a pamphlet
within the book,

Story and Souvenir of Baseball Rubbing.

It reads --
"Baseball Rubbing Clay from the Delaware River,
Burlington County, New Jersey."

Real clay.
Rubbed on baseballs.

I think of the poems
"Two On, Two Out,"

"The Reanimation of Ted Williams' Frozen Head,"

but it's the packet I shake,
hold up to the light,
press between my fingers.

It's dirt.

Not just dirt.
According to the pamphlet,
　　this sample contains
　　　　carbonaceous matter, quartz granules,
　　　　particles of feldspar and pyrite, iron oxide,
　　　　pellets of gray siderite, dark lignite coal
　　　　fragments, and finely divided mica flakes.

Who can read anything
but the story of baseball rubbing?
I toss her book to the bed.

　　　　New balls arrive at the home club in factory-
　　　　sealed packages.
　　　　Each baseball has one continuous seam of
　　　　exactly 108 double stitches.
　　　　Umpires remov[e] the gloss from the surface
　　　　of new balls, a major league rule.

I want to tear open the packet,
pour clay on my tongue to know
it won't melt like table salt,
pure cane sugar.

I want to tap the envelope
for its last grain.

I trust it's clean.

They have to know
children will want to
muddy the roofs of their mouths with it,

spit the black juice like tobacco.

Jilly would understand "The Last Big Bet"
could easily have been the certainty
of the torn and empty packet,

my black-streaked tongue and shuddering body
already filling with the earth.

I RECEIVE, DIRECTLY FROM JEANNINE HALL GAILEY, *BECOMING THE VILLAINESS*

I weighed the book in my hands,
studied the glossy cover
of a preening she-devil,
opened it, thumbed it
twice.

A tiny card flipped out,
its cover depicting the handwriting
of Isaac Newton.

Thanks for buying this,
she wrote inside,
penned her initials.

She enclosed an empty envelope
stamped with *Wonder Woman* postage –
39 cents.

I considered the superhuman strength it took
to indelibly press the letters
on each page,
times one thousand books.

I marveled
at the bionic arm required
to apply super-heated glue

to bind one thousand covers
to their contents
at hypersonic speed,

stood awestruck at the thought
of the airmail letter, arms outstretched,
and her book, that sidekick,

negotiating the airspace
of North America,
avoiding the Northeast Corridor
and Atlantic storms, the *Zugspitze*,

overflying half of Asia's dusty flats
to stick a perfect landing
in my hands.

And that thank you card,

the cape of its paper flap unfurling
to reveal,
emblazoned in red ink,

> *JHG*

centered inside a pentagonal shield
and rising, elaborate wings.

KEEPSAKES HIDDEN IN A JEWELRY BOX DISGUISED AS CATE MARVIN'S *FRAGMENT OF THE HEAD OF A QUEEN*

My CHU must be tidy -- no knickknacks, bric-a-brac,
matching *Baghdad 2003* salt and pepper shakers,
no tanned bikini babe
taped to the wall.

When I reached for *Fragment,*
it slipped from the shelf without fanfare, opened –

I gaped at its herringbone tangle
and almost worthless pennies
collecting on the felt bottom
like a brown sediment.

The paper scraps of poems written pink,
each "i" dotted with a heart.
A pair of pinking shears once
buried in a man's back.

A snippet of hair,
I was able to clip
when the head she lied off
rolled.

A shriveled petal
from an undelivered rose.

Beside her lover's diamond collar –
a plastic eyepiece
lay with a dirty picture
of a girl and pony inside.

This is not the worst thing,
she confessed.

I lowered the eyepiece,
closed the box and shelved it
because, Cate,
I am certain

it is not

the worst.

THE DAY I LOST LISA OLSTEIN'S
LOST ALPHABET IN MY CHU

I hadn't read it in weeks.
A black shadow filled
its slip on the shelf.

My room was ten by ten –

a bed, a wall locker,
foot locker, nightstand
wiped down daily.

It made no sense.
Where could it go?

There's something in a name,
my mother warned.
*On our tongues lie
the power of death and life.*

Outside, every moth I saw
twitched crushed
in a sparrow's beak

while Olstein's entomologist
spread beat-sheets,
laid pheromone traps.

In her own tiny hut

the dead spread
classified in order,
pinned to a sheet of cork
behind a plate of glass.

The paper labels reading
NOCTURNI PAPILIONIS MORS
and
ACHERONTIA ATROPOS

curled in the damp air
like a book in the rain,
its pages bloated
as a full chrysalis.

Still the moth she treasured
when she set out
with her nets and notebooks,
pens and pith helmet,
eluded her.

It drew her
like an insect to the light
where a jar waited
with its ether-sopped cotton,
screen and tissue paper.

Not one hole punched
through the lid for air.

READING LEE UPTON'S *THE INVENTION OF KINDNESS* UNTIL IT FALLS APART

I cracked *The Invention of Kindness* nightly for months
to reread "Scenes from a Bus" --

> *that common chicken there*
> *tilted over and pleased, pleased*

and another poem --

> *I have been so tired,*
> *so frightened, so sad*

as outgoing artillery shook my cot.
The lighting flickered and hummed.

I finally broke the spine.

It unraveled in my hands
as I slept.

At four a.m. I woke, discerned
strewn pages on the floor.

The empty cover perched
like a dove on my chest,

its bevy scattering
as I stumbled to the switch.

EXPLAINING WHY I BOUGHT BUT COULDN'T OPEN WELDON KEES' *COLLECTED POEMS*

You must be trained to read it.

You can't just
pick it up,
swing back a page and –

Go to town!

And I was trained.
I understood

as well as anyone the danger
of brandishing the book
while every other day
wanting to suck-start a 9mm pistol.

I recognized the apocalypse
he wrote of
on the filthy streets of Baghdad,
trash-flags flapping on the razor wire,
young men
gunning for us
nightly – their eyes
and AK-47s.

Kees' poems were sharp
as Kukri blades,
sharp as ginsu
thrust in a maple block.

So I buried them in a foot locker.

There, they would chant nothing
but a furthering
of the violence.

CIRCUMVENTING THE ARMY'S
PORNOGRAPHY BAN WITH
ANNE-MARIE LEVINE'S
BUS RIDE TO A BLUE MOVIE

It's just a slender little thing in a blue dress,
this book --
no glossy pictures
or scratch-and-sniff.

No centerfold of Anne-Marie,
her red-nailed index finger
against her candy-apple tongue.

Why would the Customs official peek inside?

He might blur the pages with his thumb,
see if acid tabs would flutter.

He never saw
how each *R* slinks her leg
around embracing *T*.
And *S*, such the contortionist --
what she can do
with an apple and bowling pins!

Night after night
my flashlight lit the screen of the page,
as I stared at the letters in their congo lines

bumping butt to groin.

Each *e* grinning
as *n*'s flat palm
swatted *d*'s bodacious ass.

DISCUSSING THE STATE OF THE WAR ON TERROR IN IRAQ WITH LAURIE SHECK'S *BLACK SERIES*

It sure is dark in here with the poisoned carpenter bees
molting in their mortis.

The mannequins are cool
as a lover's body cooled in sleep
after an evening's exertions.

I brought you here to understand
how a world clear as plate glass
could stun the errant dove in flight
and gloss itself

in siren light, then toss that sheen
like a kerchief.
to the street.

There is no answer.

Or rather
the answer is cast
in the plaster bodies of Pompeii,

swizzle stick of lightning
swirling in midnight.

We're here, and it's night.
You can't change that any more

than stuffing Medusa's head
back in its bloodied sack can revert
the most exquisite gaping statue
to the flesh.

CONTRASTING THE BATTLES IN EILEEN SILVER-LILLYWHITE'S *ALL THAT AUTUMN* WITH MY EXPERIENCES DURING OIF 2.5

What I did was a job, albeit messy
as the first slice lifted from a boysenberry pie:
I counted the dead,
captured the living,
targeted houses.

Nothing more noble than the men you observed
marching to their cars
across the pumpkin fields
after the Ford plant's midnight shift.

They slouched toward dark houses
and cold meals
or the town's last open bar.

That was the war
you reported.

While mine received the coverage,
you rubbed your wrists with ice.

We oversaw Baghdad voting.
The enemy left their guns at home and drifted
into the polling sites

to cast their ballots,
wag their purple thumbs at CNN.

Your men drilled the nearby cliffs and blew
them down for limestone.
Their hands smelled of blasting
caps and cordite.

Your grandmother toed her coffin gingerly,
that empty, tottering rowboat.
There were no hands left
to guide or spot her.

Her arms shot out for balance.

At least we knew
death sought
us.

We dressed for it daily
in helmets and armor,
goggles and gloves.

It wasn't something which suddenly tore up
and down your tree-lined, Upstate street, Eileen,
in a black Trans Am crammed
with kidnapped, screaming girls,

its laughing driver fishtailing every corner,
blowing through stop signs,
flipping off the cops.

REFLECTING ON THE CONTENTS OF MY OWN FINAL UTTERANCE AFTER READING CATHERINE PIERCE'S *FAMOUS LAST WORDS*

I think mine will be broken
by a breath,

enfolded like a matchstick
by its flaming head.

A half-sentence, words sawn
crudely as a chainsaw

strips a tree
to stumps,

though I have that final line already
fully spread and smoothed

as my best suit
on the cool bed:

the exclamation point, a paisley tie;
buttons on the gray vest,
compound verbs;

the leather belt, a list of boyhood pets;
Hound's-tooth coat, a woman's name;

socks and t-shirt;
the and *a*.

Have you ever been to Walter Reed,
Catherine?
People who thought they'd spoken

their last,
then pulled through.

It's full of sawn stumps and splintered

limbs fitted onto
the most magnificent

prosthetics.

You can hide them in a pant leg,

slip them down a sleeve.

My friend had a boss
she swore
wore a wooden leg.

She wanted me
to kick it.

She had

words laid out for me –

Did it feel like booting
a table leg?

If that was her last sentence,
what could she say

to disown it?
It would gnaw her like fire

crawling the skin
of a marshmallow.

And if I answered
laughing –

More like the solid squat
of an ottoman,

I would pray
those would not be the last

mean things I said.
But something lighthearted,

like George Appel,
strapped to the electric chair,

winking as he claimed
the witnesses soon would get a load

of a baked Appel.

Or a tantalizing fragment

I see . . .
I smell . . .
I feel . . .

my ending bequeathed to the leaning survivors
like a lump of gold

out of which could be fashioned
cufflinks, tie clip, a pinkie ring –

the ordinary, elegant items
which make the man.

AFTER READING LINDA MCCARRISTON'S *EVA-MARY,* I ACCUSE HER OF SINGLE-HANDEDLY UNDERMINING MY FOCUS DURING THE GLOBAL WAR ON TERROR

How dare you have cracked
a Soldier's bronzed patina
with the love you wrote
for an abused mother
and her children?

What makes you think
I should have looked at some
shot terrorist with pity,
a drunk hillbilly
who jokingly waved
his Glock at IPs?

You wcakcncd me every time
I spied an Iraqi child
and did not think

He's collecting intel for his father
as he signaled to us
thumbs-up.

Every time I thought
He's just a boy.

When the burqa'd woman rushed me,
hands outstretched, I sensed
she was a beggar,
not a bomber.

I pointed
dollar bills.

I saw in her the woman
of your book

fleeing her murderous husband
with her children to the flophouse,
lodging a straight-back chair
against the doorknob's brass throat
to hold at bay
  the hallway's impersonal riot.

I looked and saw
an anonymous woman trapped
in a blue net
and cotton drape.

Thanks to you I hardened
not to steel and glass
but bone and muscle.

Thanks to you
those people attained a voice

unattached to a pull ring,
unlike a mother
mute before the judge,
numb from the rifle
her husband raped her with.

You snipped their puppet strings.

The woman in your book
was snagged with her babies
in a flood.
She could not
wave in fear
of losing them.

I didn't call Iraqis
camel jockeys, rag heads, Ali Baba,
thanks to you.

I could accept
if they hated me
like the mother hated
the priest, the judge, the doctor,
those indifferent jurists.

If Afghans wanted me
pierced anus to skull
on a spit
rotating above a roasting fire,
I could accept that.

I could see my own

son balance
a soccer ball in Baghdad
on his toe,

my daughter peer tall
by the wall of Furat Mosque,
waving to patrols.

When Afghan children celebrated
Ramadan in the streets,
I reported,

Their guns are plastic toys.

And they were.

No one got shot
that night, Linda.

Thanks to you.

I GET JEN BERVIN'S *NETS*

I get it. I get the girders she bared in the sonnets
to expose their rusting underpinnings,

just as the Humvees we drove
were stripped of anything soft,
anything but the mechanical rattle
you'd expect in a war machine.

I get the bleached bones of it.

She burned the tents
down to the frames.

Bring only what you need.

I get the skeletons
collecting themselves,
moonlight gleaming off
their cranial helmets,
concentric rings of their ribs
like stacked halos.

Who has need,
they sing,

of the worthless drapes of flesh?

MY DISCUSSION WITH
SERGEANT BRIAN TURNER,
3BCT/2ID

I didn't read *Here, Bullet*.
I saw the movie.

I waited at midnight for choppers.

I patrolled the dusty street

in an iron coffin
ready-made.

As it closed
I felt the pressure

push my ear drums in.

I bought the movie soundtrack --

*the single bass drum strike
of a rocket,*

staccato roll of a SAW,

snare of approaching Chinooks.

I pined for the poster

screwed behind a cracked sheet of Plexiglas
outside the boarded theater.

I spied the decapitated tanks
hauled by the lowboys

pass through the camp
under cover of darkness.

I remember detainees
sitting all night

by the Humvees
zip-tied at the wrists.

A combat bandage served as a blind.

And when we were done

we packed up our toys
and went home.

I lounged in the APOD,
listened to my IPOD.

I flipped up a screen,
whipped out a movie.

I saw that movie.

I read the book.

WHAT I WANTED FROM ANN HUDSON'S BOOK OF POETRY *THE ARMILLARY SPHERE*

Sing me a story.
Tell me a song.

I need to become
unburdened.

Sit in my tent and recite
details of a life not mine
you lived in America.

Gesture with your paper hands
at the point where your mother viewed
Julia Child on her tiny black and white,
tossed her own
> *raisins*
> *in the casserole.*

Smile as you describe
the daughters of chemical engineers
watching their fathers take knives
to divide spaghetti.
Tell me a story.
Sing me a song,

not of my U.S.,
the one which sent me here,

but yours. You know --

where a woman peers from her window
to spy the streetlights idly tossing
their green nets at midnight,

and the dream carp rise to kiss
that pond where air and water mesh,
calmly sweeping aside
the descending quadrants.

MY WARTIME E-MAIL CORRESPONDENCE WITH KELLI RUSSELL AGODON

It wasn't engaging or worthy of books --
no revealing letters of the like
between Dickinson and Colonel Higginson.

I don't recall her salutations
or closings.

Something like
Hi and

All the best.

No secrets passed
or dreams related.

No flowery allusions
to Wordsworth,
Walter Scott.

Just a common refrain --
Reread this aloud for music

or --
This part sounds a little rough

and later --
Could you tighten this stanza?

Nothing I would hide
from my wife.

It was like receiving
short transmission bursts
while strapped in a space capsule.

Roger

This is Mission Control

Even static hiss.

That evidence not of life alone
but knowledge.

Someone understanding
and relaying the vitals
of propulsion, oxygen,

the exacting principles
to guide me finally spinning
safely to the sea
in sight of the giant, watchful ships.

ON DISCOVERING J. ALLYN ROSSER'S POEM "EARLY IN ANY CENTURY" IN THE CAMP VICTORY RECREATION CENTER DONATED BOOK LIBRARY

Among ten thousand black and broken spines,
amid the pulpy waves
of Susan Grisham and Zane Gray,
Stephen King and Barbara Cartland,
there floating

on

one of fifty sagging shelves –
The Georgia Review.

I waded its contents, discovered
Rosser's poem.

I read it.

I read it
four times straight
and I wanted
to take it, but --

the volume

would not fit
in my pocket.
I considered slitting the page.
A soldier sat nearby.

I read it again,
returned it to the shelf.

I thought of the path
the poem took,

the path
I took
to read it.

A raft and lifeboat
converging on the sea.

The exhausted passengers waved
and, closing,
asked alike for water.

Having none to give,
they leaned in anyway
across the gap
to touch

and release
each other's
disbelieving hand.

HOW BETH BACHMANN'S *TEMPER* AND KATHLEEN SHEEDER BONANNO'S *SLAMMING OPEN THE DOOR* CHANGED MY LIFE

Have you ever been lost,
so lost the maps you held
gave no hint of place,

and the road
was stark as a black ribbon
cinching a box of dust?

When I held the broken compass to my chest,
loss' azimuth adjusted.

The needle spun
fast as the wheel on the Game of Life.

Clouds obscured the sun,
shadows refused me
North.

I littered the nearby earth
with crooked sundials.

I read
    The head is damaged and cannot read this image

and understood
  can you tell me
  where to turn.

This was not a question
but a discerning of vultures
in the haze.

What they eyed so keenly
from the updraft
in this country pocked with death

must have been human
though it collapsed on itself now
like a ransacked city,

ribs of the dead
arching the doors of the houses,
femurs studding the walls.

I CONSIDER SIMILARITIES
BETWEEN BAGHDAD'S
AL-FURAT MOSQUE AND THE
DRESDNER FRAUENKIRCHE
AFTER READING CYNTHIA
MARIE HOFFMAN'S *SIGHTSEER*

The mosque resembles
    not at all
the soaring Frauenkirche,
Athassel Priory,
    nor even
the gleaming ruins
of Hoare Abbey.

War is all they share,

that, and fists of frightened women
pounding heavy doors.

The mosque squats
beneath its dome of mud
sculpted the shape and color
of a Vidalia onion.

It barely clears the ten-foot wall
topped with razor wire
enclosing it.

Tank tracks rut the nearby mud.

I'm not a tourist.
I'm hunched in a Humvee
armed and draped
with fifty pounds of armor.

I'm not stopping to admire
the inner ablution font
or qiblah wall.

I couldn't enter
if I wanted to view
the ornate musalla
or raised minbar,
discern *Allah*
amid the calligraphic Arabic.

In a second
we pass
its burr of doves which lift as one
disintegrating sheet
before a pair of passing choppers,

the sound of their rotors
slapping against the mosque
like a panicked woman
finding the doors
locked, and bolted, and chained.

THE BOOKS I BROUGHT TO READ WHILE FLYING HOME

Leaving Iraq for good,
we lined our packs by the chopper pad,
awaited the Chinooks.

In mine, atop the uniforms and extra boots
I tucked two books
for the transatlantic trip:
Digges' *Vesper Sparrows*,
Behn's *Paper Bird*.

I *needed* them.

Gulf Air flights only aired two flicks:
The Sands of Iwo Jima
and *Jarhead*.
We weren't even Marines.

So when the Chinooks arrived
and hovered above the pad,
the packs tipped and ripped open.

I watched my books
flap and catch and rise
on the rotor wash,
then explode in twin turbine back blast --

flushed doves wheeling

before their white feathers
burst on the wind.

NOTES

The original idea for this book germinated with the concept behind Lynn Butler's volume of poetry *Planting the Voice: Poems from Poems* (University of Central Florida Press, 1989).

CHU stands for *containerized housing unit*, a trailer housing Soldiers in Iraq and Afghanistan.

Lisa Olstein's opening quote is from an interview with Robert Casper of *jubilat,* in 2006.

"Harriet Rubin's Mother's Wooden Hand" is the namesake poem in Susan Hahn's book, found on pp. 8 in the volume. A "one-oh-seven" refers to a 107 millimeter rocket, commonly used by Iraqi and Afghan insurgents to strike American bases and other fixed sites.

Excerpts in "A Soldier Loans Me Her Copy of Sylvia Plath's *The Collected Poems*," are from "Burning the Letters," pp. 204, "The Applicant," pp. 221, "Lady Lazarus," pp. 244 and "The Couriers," pp. 247. A thank you to Danielle Palace Blanco for inspiring this poem.

The excerpt in "Romancing Christine Garren's *Among the Monarchs* despite Central Command's General Order 1" is from "Noon," pp. 21. The close is inspired by "The Laboratory," pp. 48.

Excerpted lines in "Finding What in Rachel Contreni Flynn's *Ice, Mouth, Song* Brings Me to Conclude it is Oracular" are from "Daughters," pp. 16, "State Home, 1984," pp. 31-32, "The Trap," pp. 53, "Nerve Gas Warehouse," pp. 36, "Black Appendix," pp. 41-44, "I Will Not be Sad in This World," pp. 68-69, and "Still Slipping," pp. 58.

Poems mentioned or referenced in "Kathleen Graber's *Correspondence* Gives Me a Paper Cut After a Hard Day in Iraq" are on pp. 4-5, 14-17, 26-27, 30-33, 48-50, 63-65 and 73-76.

Excerpts in "At the End of the Day, I Get Creeped Out by Louise Gluck's Detached Tone in *Ararat*," are from "A Fantasy," pp. 16-17.

The reference to Ethel Rosenberg in "What was I Thinking, Bringing Adrienne Rich's *A Wild Patience Has Taken Me This Far*?" is from "For Ethel Rosenberg," pp. 26-30. My line "dove into the wreck" is based off the title of her book *Diving Into the Wreck*.

Excerpts in "Yusuf Komunyakaa's Book *Dien Cai Dau* Assumes the Role of Commiserating Old Soldier," starting with "this one," are from Yusuf Komunyakaa's book *Dien Cai Dau*: "Missing in Action," pp. 59-60; "Thanks," pp. 44-5; "Short Timer's Calendar," pp. 43; "Night Muse & Mortar Round," pp. 21; "Tunnels," pp. 5-6; "Communiqué," pp. 30-1; and "A Break from the Bush," pp. 27.

Kristin Hersh's song "In Shock" is from her album

Learn to Sing Like a Star.

The excerpted line in "Christianne Balk and I Discuss Snipe Hunting while Reading Her Book *Bindweed*" is from "Before I Learned to Say Goodbye," pp. 46-50.

The excerpted lines in "Lynda Hull Raises *Ghost Money* to Haunt Me Over There" are from "1933," pp. 9-11, and "Tide of Voices," pp. 3-5.

"The Two-Headed Calf" is on pp. 59, while "Seeing a Dog in the Rain" is found on pp. 71, in Laura Gilpin's Walt Whitman Award Winning Book of Poems for 1976, (Selected by William Stafford) *The Hocus-Pocus of the Universe.*

Excerpts in "I Get my Messiah Complex On with Cynthia Zarin's *Fire Lyric*" are from "Recollection," pp. 59, and "Song," pp. 71.

Excerpts in "The Commanding Presence of Karen Fish's *The Cedar Canoe*" are from "Crossing," pp. 45-46 and "Approximation," pp. 3. The paraphrased line "Cool as precious metal" is inspired by "The Orchard," pp. 12.

Excerpts in "Jilly Dybka Sends Me the Dirt on Baseballs Inside a Copy of *Trouble and Honey*" are from *Story and Souvenir of Baseball Rubbing*, © 1970, by The Company of Young Salesmen, Bloomington, Minnesota.

The disparate themes connecting "Keepsakes Hidden

in a Jewelry Box Disguised as Cate Marvin's *Fragment of the Head of a Queen*" are from pp. 13-14, "Lines for a Mentor," pp. 22-23, "Gaslight," pp. 46-48, "Lying My Head Off," pp. 24-26, "My Black Address," pp. 54-55, "A Brief Attachment," and, pp. 27-28, as well as the italicized line, from "Teens Love Horse Dick."

Excerpts in "Reading Lee Upton's *The Invention of Kindness* until it Falls Apart" are from "Scenes from a Bus," pp. 3-4 and "Suddenly the Late Show," pp. 28-29.

Paraphrased themes in "Discussing the State of the War on Terror in Iraq with Laurie Sheck's Book *Black Series*" are from "The Carpenter Bees," pp. 50-51, "The Mannequins," pp. 12-13, "The Store Windows Glitter," pp. 3-4, "Pompeii, pp. 30, "Summer Storm," pp. 78-79, and "Medusa," pp. 18-19.

Paraphrased ideas within "Contrasting the Battles in Eileen Silver-Lillywhite's *All That Autumn* with my Experiences During OIF 2.5" are from "All That Autumn," pp. 3, "The Summer Bruce Died," pp. 6-7, "Rain," pp. 5, and "My Grandmother's Funeral," pp. 56. OIF 2.5 occurred between June 2004 and June 2005 in Iraq. OIF is short for Operation Iraqi Freedom.

The portion addressing George Appel in "Reflecting on my own Final Utterance After Reading Catherine Pierce's *Famous Last Words*" is from "Well, Gentlemen, You Are About to See a Baked Appel," pp. 58-59.

Paraphrased themes from "After Reading Linda McCarriston's *Eva-Mary*, I Accuse Her of Single

Handedly Undermining My Focus During the Global War on Terror" come from "Hotel Nights with my Mother," pp. 24-5, "To Judge Faolain, Dead Long Enough: A Summons," pp. 12-3 and "My Mother's Chair: 1956, pp. 18-9. The line "the hallway's impersonal riot" is also from "Hotel Nights with my Mother." IP stands for Iraqi Police.

2BCT/3ID stands for Second Brigade Combat Team/ Third Infantry Division, the unit in which Brian Turner served as a sergeant in Iraq. SAW is short for squad automatic weapon, a light machinegun. APOD stands for Air Point of Debarkation, an airfield where Soldiers redeploy to the United States from the Middle East.

The excerpt in "What I Needed from Ann Hudson's Book of Poems *The Armillary Sphere*" is from "Ode to Julia Child," pp. 24. Paraphrased lines and ideas are from pp. 23, 24, 37 and 54.

The first italicized line in "How Beth Bachmann's *Temper* and Kathleen Sheeder Bonanno's *Slamming Open the Door* Changed My Life" is from "Plot," in *Temper*, pp. 16. The second italicized line is from "Red Saturn," in *Slamming Open the Door*, pp. 31.

The italicized line in "Thank you, Jennifer Kronovet's *Awayward*, for Rescuing Me, is from the poem "The Shallow Sun of It," pp. 73.

REFERENCES

Agodon, Kelli Russell, *Small Knots*. Cherry Grove Collections, 2004.

Bachmann, Beth, *Temper*. University of Pittsburgh Press, 2009.

Balk, Christianne, *Bindweed*. Collier Books, 1986.

Behn, Robin, *Paper Bird*. Texas Tech University Press, 1988.

Bervin, Jen, *Nets*. Ugly Duckling Presse, 2004.

Bonanno, Kathleen Sheeder, *Slamming Open the* Door. Alice James Press, 2009.

Butler, Lynn, *Planting the Voice: Poems from Poems*. Univ. of Central Florida Press, 1989.

Digges, Debra, *Vespar Sparrows*. Knopf, 2001.

Dybka, Jilly, *Trouble and Honey*. Bear Shirt Press, 2009.

Fish, Karen, *The Cedar Canoe*. University of Georgia Press, 1987.

Flynn, Rachel Contreni, *Ice, Mouth, Song*. Tupelo Press, 2005.

Gailey, Jeannine Hall, *Becoming the Villainess*. Steel Toe Press, 2006.

Garren, Christine, *Among the Monarchs*. University of Chicago Press, 2000.

Gilpin, Laura, *The Hocus-Pocus of the Universe*. Doubleday & Company, 1977.

Gluck, Louise, *Ararat*. Ecco Press, 1990.

Graber, Kathleen, *Correspondence*. Saturnalia Books, 2005.

Hahn, Susan, *Harriet Rubin's Mother's Wooden Hand*. University of Chicago Press, 1988.

Hersh, Kristin, *Learn to Sing Like a Star*, Yep Roc Records, 2007.

Hoffman, Cynthia Marie, *Sightseer*. Persea Books, 2010.

Hudson, Ann, *The Armillary Sphere*. Ohio University Press, 2006.

Hull, Lynda, *Ghost Money*. University of Massachusetts Press, 1986.

Kees, Weldon, *Collected Poems*. University of Nebraska Press, 1975.

Komunyakaa, Yusuf, *Dien Cai Dau*. Wesleyan University Press, 1988.

Kronovet, Jennifer, *Awayward*. BOA Ltd., 2009.

Levine, Anne-Marie, *Bus Ride to a Blue Movie*. Pearl Editions, 2003.

Marvin, Cate, *Fragment of the Head of a Queen*. BOA Ltd., 2008.

McCarriston, Linda, *Eva-Mary*. Triquarterly Books, 1991.

McCaslin, Susan, *Flying Wounded*. University Press of Florida, 2000.

Olstein, Lisa, *Lost Alphabet*. Copper Canyon, 2009.

Pierce, Catherine, *Famous Last Words*. Saturnalia Books, 2008.

Plath, Sylvia, *The Collected Poems*. Harper & Row, 1981.

Rich, Adrienne, *A Wild Patience Has Taken Me This Far*. W.W. Norton & Co., 1981.

Rosser, J. Allyn, *Bright Moves*. Northeastern University Press, 1986.

Sheck, Laurie, *Black Series*. Knopf, 2001.

Silver-Lillywhite, Eileen, *All That Autumn*. Ithaca House Press, 1983.

Turner, Brian, *Here, Bullet*. Alice James Press, 2008.

Upton, Lee, *The Invention of Kindness*. University of Alabama Press, 1987.

Zarin, Cynthia, *Fire Lyric*. Knopf, 1993.

THANK YOU, JENNIFER KRONOVET'S *AWAYWARD*, FOR RESCUING ME!

Jesus saves.

And He will come.

But on a day I thought I must
end my life, I didn't turn
to *John* or *Romans* or *Job*.

I didn't see
my life was rocking and creaking
along some crumbling precipice.

I read instead *Awayward*.

Jennifer Kronovet,
what could you say but

> *I don't know how to say it.*
> *Just bye. Or bye bye.*

I mean, this is life, isn't it?

Your poems weren't designed
to yank a man off a ledge,
to smack him from his hysterics.

232

But they did,

and you turned away
when I was safe and grateful,

your work done
like any hero.
No talking,
no smiling.

The palms inside your gleaming gloves
were red from all that slapping.